Who Won?
The 2024 Presidential Election

By
Tom McAuliffe

Next Stop Paradise Publishing
Fort Walton Beach, Florida, USA

Who Won?
The 2024 Presidential Election

by Tom McAuliffe

First EDITION - 2024

For more information email:
bookinfo@nextstopparadise.com

WWW.AUTHORTOMMCAULIFFE.COM

<u>Dedications</u>

To the Election Workers of America

To Anyone who Voted

**100% of the Profits of this book will be
donated to The League of Women Voters**

BLUE   RED

6

TABLE OF CONTENTS

PREFACE

For most of us, Election Day marks a welcome end to months of relentless political ads and partisan bickering. You show up at your polling place, run the gantlet of sign-wielding campaign volunteers, and join your fellow Americans in long lines that inch toward the voting booth. Most are fully electronic while others give the illusion of old time paper ballots yet are still fed into a digital tabulation machine. Maybe you while away the time quietly reflecting on the choices you're about to make. Sadly these days expressing one's political opinion can lead to real challenges, Social exile and sometimes even violence.

And sometimes one doesn't need to say anything... as I stood in line to vote one woman was wearing a button that declared: 'VOTE—your vagina is counting on you!' Another had a T-shirt supporting Harris and red MAGA hats were everywhere. I was in deep red NW Florida the land of conservative rabble rouser Congressman Matt Gatez and GOP Governor Ron Desantis and here folks can talk politics anywhere and carry a gun everywhere! Unlike Florida, many states have laws against passive electioneering, such as wearing political buttons or T-shirts within a certain distance of the voting machines—usually the demarcation is within 100-150 feet. In 2008 when a 9-year-old girl accompanied her Mom to the polls wearing an

Obama T-shirt, an election judge intercepted them and told the girl to turn the shirt inside out.

Still, electioneering laws differ and enforcement can be spotty, says Elisabeth MacNamara, national President of the League of Women Voters. "It varies from state to state and even from county to county," MacNamara says. "Even what steps a poll worker takes [to prevent electioneering] vary by state."

As originally ratified in the U.S. Constitution each state was granted the right to determine voting qualifications for its residents. After the Civil War, there were three Reconstruction amendments that limited voting rights. The 15th Amendment, passed in 1870, was the most important providing that "[t]he right of citizens of the United States to vote shall not be denied or abridged by the United States or by any State on account of race, color, or previous condition of servitude. "Years later Women were first allowed to vote after an uphill fight and finally the passage of the 19th Amendment in 1920.

Blacks in southern states unfortunately we not so luck as local governments actively sought to disenfranchise racial minorities who tried to exercise their right to vote. Intimidation, outright voter fraud and so-called "Jim Crow Laws," which imposed voting restrictions like literacy tests, property ownership requirements, poll taxes, etc., were used to severely limit African American participation in the voting processes of the southland. It worked. In North Carolina, not a single Black voter was eligible to vote in any election from 1896 until 1904. In Louisiana, only 730 Black voters were registered to vote statewide in 1904—less than 0.5% of the Black male population at that time. Alabama? Georgia? Mississippi? The same.

The Civil Rights Act of 1964, which outlawed discrimination in public accommodations such as hotels, restaurants and other businesses, and followed by the Voting Rights Act of 1965, essentially eliminated legally sanctioned state barriers to voting for all federal, state and local elections. These were landmark pieces of legislation which finally ended a shameful era of disenfranchisement of minorities in the south. Nevertheless, federal oversight of some local areas with historically low voter turnout was still necessary, as people can be very creative in their attempts to obtain and hold onto political power. Section 5 of the Voting Rights Act of 1965 required that certain states and local governments require a "pre-clearance" from the U.S. Attorney General's office to insure that that changes to their voting laws or practices do not "deny or abridge the right to vote on account of race, color, or membership in a language minority group" before those changes may be enforced. And while even today some voter suppression occurs we are far better off than when we started on the road to a 'More perfect union.'

Fast forward 50 years and in the wake of the 2016 election, when Russian, Chinese and Iranian operatives attempted to breach the U.S. voting system, many states, took steps to ensure the integrity of their voting processes. The problem was the new rules and requirements disenfranchise voters of color. Add to that the atmosphere of distrust that has been sown. After losing as the 2020 election results unfolded, President Donald Trump took the extraordinary step of insisting that there had been widespread election fraud. It was the first time in American history that a Presidential candidate refused to concede and wish their opponent well in governing our nation. And true or not, our nation's political discourse will probably never be the same. God help us if we can't put the pieces back together. But I believe we can and will.

This book documents the 2024 election as well as addressing the current state of our politics. As background I have been involved in politics since I was a teenager and was a supporter of Minnesota's Hubert Humphrey. Later I helped run Presidential candidate Gary Harts campaign in NW Florida and

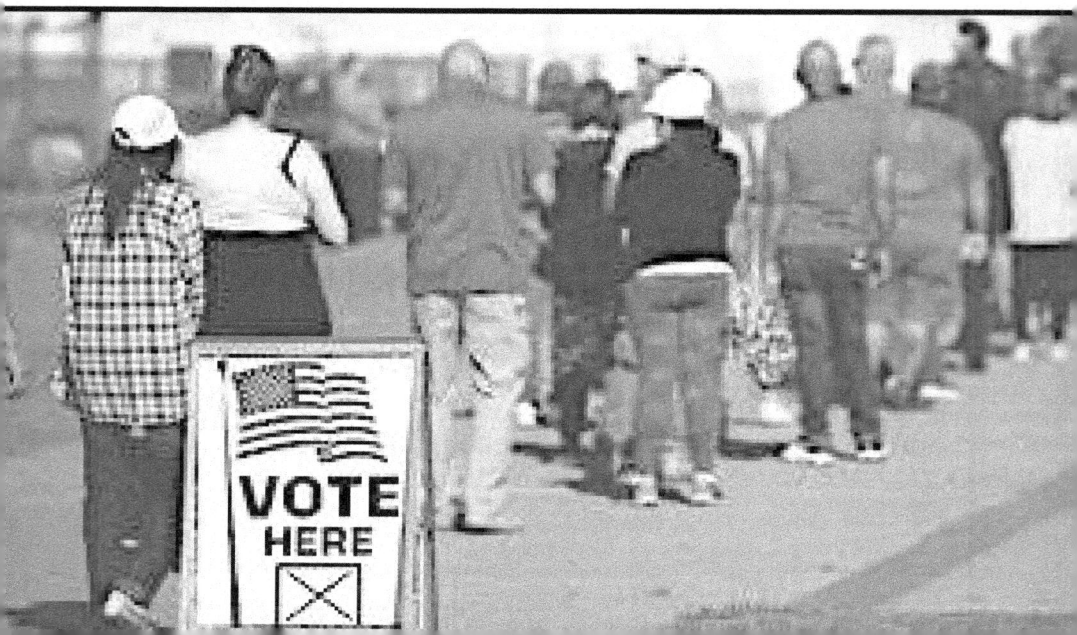

then served as a percent captain for California house Speaker Willie Brown in the 16th District in San Francisco, More recently I served at the Hawaii State Legislature and ran the campaign of the first Latino woman to run for the Florida House of Representatives. While we lost we did get more votes than any other Democrat candidate who had ever run in NW Florida. Man or woman. The race reinforced to me the inequities of our current system and how divided we have become, And it's not just with politics although that is the tip of it… but over all we have lost the art of conversation in this country. Gone are the days when we could agree to disagree without thinking that the other person was evil and hates America.

And what is indeed a shame became while we argue about kneeling during the nation anthem, what is free speech or when life begins, our nation now has significant and fundamental challenges that must be addressed. If they aren't it is not hyperbole to say that our country's days may be numbered. Not saying that we would cease to exists but the country we grew up in would be no longer. We must find a way to bridge the gap not just politically, although that is vitally important, but also communicatively. We must learn how to talk to each other again.

Let the conversation begin…

Tom

CHAPTER 1

Understanding Our Voting System
The Foundation of Democracy

The United States voting system is a fundamental aspect of American democracy, designed to give citizens a voice in government and ensure representation. It operates on both state and federal levels, with elections for positions ranging from local mayors to the President of the United States. However, the mechanics of the system are more complex than simply casting a ballot. To understand how the U.S. voting system works, we must examine the structure, processes, and rules that govern elections in this vast, diverse country.

One of the defining characteristics of the U.S. voting system is its de-centralized nature, rooted in federalism. While federal laws establish basic voting rights, most of the authority over how elections are run is vested in individual states. This means that every state has the power to set its own rules about who can vote, how votes are cast, and how elections are conducted, within the framework of the U.S. Constitution and federal law.

When it comes too voting its all about state control. Each state determines election procedures, voter registration methods, and voting locations, resulting in different systems across the country. There are various election types... Voters participate in federal, state, and local elections, including presidential, congressional, gubernatorial, and municipal races. This decentralization allows for flexibility and state autonomy but can also result in confusion for voters, particularly during presidential elections when voting rules differ dramatically from state to state.

One of the most distinctive features of the U.S. voting system is the Electoral College, used only in presidential elections. Rather than being decided by a simple popular vote, the outcome of the presidential election is determined by electors chosen by each state. It is one of the most misunderstood aspects of the American voting system. Each state is allocated a number of electoral votes based on its representation in Congress (the sum of its Senators and House Representatives). It's a winner-takes-all system and in most states, the candidate who wins the popular vote in the state secures all of that state's electoral votes (with the exceptions of Maine and Nebraska, which allocate votes proportionally).

The 270 Threshold: A candidate must win a majority of the 538 electoral votes—at least 270—to secure the presidency. This system can result in situations where a candidate wins the presidency without winning the national popular vote, as occurred in 2000 and 2016. While the Electoral College is a cornerstone of the U.S. system, it remains a subject of debate regarding its fairness and relevance in modern elections.

Not just anyone can vote there is a Voter Registration system that insures eligibility. Voting is not automatic, and citizens must actively register to vote. Voter registration rules are governed by state law and can vary widely across the country.

To be eligible to vote, a person must be a U.S.

citizen, at least 18 years old, and meet state residency requirements. Some states restrict voting rights for individuals convicted of felonies, though this varies by jurisdiction. There are various Registration methods. Citizens can register through a variety of means, including online systems, mail-in forms, and in-person registration at designated offices or during events like voter drives. Many states have adopted automatic voter registration

The very first Electoral College

through the Department of Motor Vehicles (DMV) or other agencies. States also set specific deadlines for voter registration, which vary but often close weeks before an election. They also offer different voting accommodations, such as same-day registration, for individuals who miss these deadlines, although this is not universal.

When it comes to the actual voting methods it's varied from paper Ballots to electronic Booths and touch screens. The method of casting a vote in U.S. elections has evolved significantly over our nations history. Today, voters can typically cast their ballots in three main ways:

•In-Person Voting: On Election Day, voters can go to polling places to cast their ballots. Polling places are usually set up in schools, community centers, or other public buildings, and voting is supervised by election officials to ensure fairness.

•Early Voting: Many states offer early voting, allowing voters to cast their ballots in person during a specific period before Election Day. This is designed to reduce congestion at polling places and provide more flexibility for voters.

•Absentee & Mail-In Voting: Absentee voting allows those who cannot make it to the polls on Election Day to vote by mail. Some states have expanded this option to include all voters (sometimes referred to as universal mail-in voting), while others restrict it to certain categories, such as the elderly, military personnel, or those with disabilities.

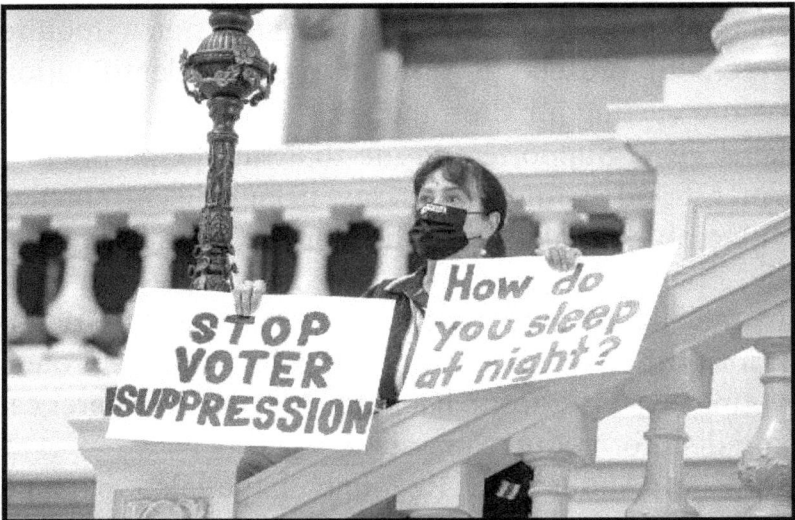

The methods available to voters can differ significantly from state to state, and recent elections have seen an increasing reliance on mail-in ballots, particularly during times of crisis like the COVID pandemic.

The emphasis at efforts to safeguard our elections are relatively recent. The integrity of U.S. elections has become a central issue, particularly in recent years. Statistics show that voter fraud occurs in only .0025% of election cycles. Ensuring that every vote is counted accurately, while protecting against fraud or interference, it is critical to maintaining public trust in the system. There are new Voter ID Laws that attempt to address this. Many states require voters to present a form of picture identification before casting a ballot, though the specifics of these laws vary. Supporters argue that this helps prevent voter fraud, while critics say it can disenfranchise vulnerable populations who don't have that type of ID. Election Security has also come to the forefront. In the digital age, cybersecurity has become a top priority. State and federal officials work to protect voting systems from hacking, foreign interference, and disinformation campaigns.

Built in Audits and Recounts have also become more commonplace. After elections, states often conduct audits or recounts, especially in close races, to verify the accuracy of the vote count. Sometimes automatically. These procedures are essential in ensuring transparency and public trust in the electoral process.

In U.S. elections, political parties play a significant role in shaping the choices available to voters. The two-party system dominates, with the Democratic and Republican parties consistently fielding candidates for most offices, although third-party candidates occasionally have a presence.

Before the general election, primary elections or caucuses are held within each party to select their candidate. These can be closed (only registered party members can vote) or open (voters can choose which primary to participate in, regardless of party affiliation). The national conventions of each party are significant political events where the chosen nominee is officially announced, and party platforms are outlined. Sometimes there are third parties.

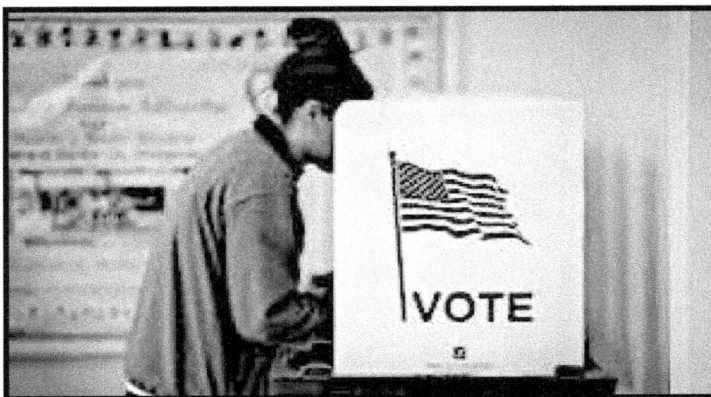

While third-party candidates rarely win national elections, they can impact the results by siphoning votes from major party candidates.

Ours is a complex and evolving system. The U.S. voting system, with its layers of federalism, local control, and historical quirks like the Electoral College, can be both empowering and perplexing. While it allows for state flexibility and citizen involvement, the complexities can lead to confusion and unequal access to the ballot. Understanding how it works is crucial for navigating the evolving landscape of American democracy and participating fully in the process.

As debates over election laws, voter access, and the future of the Electoral College continue, the core mission of the U.S. voting system remains clear: to ensure that every citizen has a voice in their government. One person. One Vote. All counted. Sounds simple doesn't it?

CHAPTER 2

Every 4 Years
The Circus Comes To Town

The craziness descends upon the nation every 4 years like a reoccurring locus. It was early September, and the nation was already buzzing. The Election was right around the corner… a year and a half from now! Across the country, lawn signs were popping up like weeds after a summer rainstorm, TV ads were running on a loop, and political commentators were shouting at each other across split screens. Election season in America isn't just an event—it's a spectacle, a marathon with sprints, a national obsession that consumes everything in its path for the better part of a year. Every four years,

the country descended into a kind of organized chaos, and 2024 was no different.

The airwaves were filled with campaign slogans, promises, and accusations. It didn't matter if you lived in the heart of a city or the middle of nowhere; there was no escaping it. Coffee shops buzzed with heated debates, dinner tables were battlegrounds, and neighbors who'd been friendly for years were now suddenly at odds over bumper stickers on their cars. And it wasn't even Election Day yet.

Like clockwork, every four years America throws itself into the political fire, burning hotter as the months roll by. The sheer intensity is overwhelming. This time there was something absurdly surreal about how the fabric of everyday life seemed to unravel bit by bit as the election cycle ramped up.

The candidates themselves were already caricatures before the general public ever really got to know them. Their lives, their families, their childhood traumas, and their college scandals were all meticulously dissected under the glaring lights of

the 24-hour news cycle. Everyone had a past, and it was all up for grabs. In the age of social media, every tweet, every offhand comment, every college photo at a party became a topic for national debate. And while some viewed it as democracy in action, others saw it for what it often felt like—a circus.

The debates were the height of the madness. What had once been a serious platform for candidates to discuss issues had transformed into a gladiatorial spectacle, where points were scored not on substance, but on zingers. The moderators were more like referees, occasionally stepping in to break up verbal fights but mostly allowing the combatants to tear each other apart.

In the first debate of 2024, two moderators had struggled to keep control as President Biden and former President Trump bickered over everything from foreign policy to the color of their opponents' ties. One candidate, a career politician known for his sharp wit, was interrupted so many times that the moderator, in an exasperated voice, finally asked, "Can you please let him finish?" It became a meme within minutes. The internet lit up with GIFs and remixes of the moment, but no one remembered what policies had been discussed.

There were dozens of these moments—gaffes, zingers, and personal attacks. A viral video of one candidate yelling over another racked up millions of views. Comment sections were flooded with armchair experts dissecting every word, every raised eyebrow. Pundits, both professional and amateur, dissected every moment of the debates as if they were sacred texts.

The performance of President Biden forced him to leave the race and support VP Harris who took over without missing a beat. The second debate was a complete reversal with the incumbent VP winning handily. Her experience as a DA proved valuable.

Social media was the new battlefield, where every post was weaponized, and nothing was off-limits. Misinformation, conspiracy theories, and doctored videos blurred the line between truth and fiction. People were no longer just voters—they were participants in a virtual war, choosing sides and lobbing digital grenades at anyone who dared disagree.

The campaign trail is its own kind of madness. Candidates crisscrossed the country in planes, buses, and caravans, appearing in diners in Iowa one day and in front of the Capitol Building the next. No hand went unshaken, no baby unkissed, no small-town dinner or fair unvisited. Every gesture was choreographed for the cameras. Every smile was calculated to appear both genuine and... Presidential.

The candidates spoke in soundbites, designed not to communicate policy but to ensure they were trending on social media. Reporters asked questions, but the real goal wasn't to provide answers—it was to create moments. Because, in the American election cycle, moments were currency.

In the frantic sprint to gain attention, candidates outdid themselves. One contender famously downed a cheeseburger in front of a cheering crowd at a state fair, only to later be caught on a hot mic confessing that he was a vegan. It didn't matter; the image of him biting into that burger circulated for weeks, endearing him to middle America.

Rallies turned into shows. Lights, music, and flag-waving crowds became the backdrop for speeches filled with promises, few of which would ever come to fruition. But no one cared about that. It was about the energy, the passion, the spectacle. It was about watching someone stand on a stage and shout into a microphone about how things would be different—this time. It was a show, and every four years, the audience came back for more.

Attack ads hit the airwaves early in the cycle (sometimes as early as a full year before!), and they didn't stop until Election Day. Slickly produced 30-second spots saturated television and radio, portraying opponents in the most unflattering light possible. Slow-motion shots of candidates looking stern or flustered played alongside ominous music, while voiceovers asked, "Is this who you want leading the country?" It didn't matter if the allegations were true. The goal wasn't truth—it was to plant doubt.

Outrage sold, and every political campaign knew it. Attack ads weren't just an occasional tactic; they were the foundation of modern campaigning. The ads came so thick and fast that voters became numb to them. One week, it was revelations about tax returns; the next, it was an ancient photo from a fraternity party. Each new scandal barely had time to breathe before it was replaced by another.

Cable news only fanned the flames, giving airtime to the most sensational stories. In an era of dwindling attention spans, news had to shock to survive. Each network catered to its own echo chamber, fueling the divisions that already existed. It wasn't about informing the public; it was about keeping viewers glued to their screens, waiting for the next scandal to break.

Talk radio, podcasts, and political blogs added to the noise. Everyone had an opinion, and every opinion had a platform. The sheer volume of content was staggering. The truth was often drowned out by the sheer number of voices shouting over one another.

Polls are the sacred texts of election cycles. Pollsters seemed to release new data every day, tracking every possible demographic slice of the electorate. How were suburban mothers in Ohio leaning this week? What about retirees in Florida? Were Latinos in Arizona shifting toward one candidate or the other? Every shift, no matter how small, was analyzed to death.

The polling frenzy had an almost hypnotic effect. Pundits and analysts dissected the data with a zeal usually reserved for religious scholars. A one-point swing in a key battleground state could lead to hours of breathless speculation on cable news. But polls were as fickle as the voters they tracked, and everyone knew that a lead today could evaporate tomorrow.

There was something oddly comforting about the constant polling updates. It gave the illusion of control in an election cycle that often felt unmoored from reality. But the reliance on polls also created a bizarre narrative loop: polls influenced voter perception, which in turn influenced future polls. It was a cycle of self-perpetuating uncertainty.

Election night is supposed to be the climax—the moment when the madness finally ends and the country can exhale and join together to wish the new President well. Fat chance! But, as had become the norm in the past few election cycles, Election Night was just the beginning of another kind of insanity… the long wait for results.

As more states adopted mail-in and early voting, the process of counting votes stretched from hours to days, sometimes even weeks. In 2024, the wait was agonizingly slow. Cable news kept rolling live coverage, showing maps with constantly shifting colors, pundits debating exit polls, and anchors trying to maintain composure as the clock ticked past midnight. Sleep-deprived correspondents stood outside election offices, reporting on every batch of votes as if they were vital updates from the front lines of a war. And in a way they are.

Social media erupted with conspiracy theories and baseless claims of fraud, fueling an already charged atmosphere. Each new update from battleground states was dissected in real time by thousands of amateur analysts, each convinced they knew more than the professionals. Accusations flew, protests erupted, and tensions mounted. For many, the waiting was unbearable.

And when the results finally trickled in, one state at a time, there was no sweeping moment of catharsis —just exhaustion. The country had once again been through the wringer, and the fatigue was palpable. Both parties let loose the Lawyers.

When the dust settled, America found itself in a familiar place: a nation deeply divided, unsure of how to move forward. The election had been won, but victory didn't bring any peace. There were calls for unity, but no one really believed it is possible. The wounds are too fresh, the scars from the campaign too deep. No voter wants to admit a wrong vote and nobody wants a finger wagging in their face.

For the losing side, there was bitterness and anger. For the winners, a hollow sense of triumph. Everyone knew that the cycle would begin again in four years, perhaps sooner, and the madness would return. America had become a country that couldn't escape its cycle of political insanity. The election cycle became more than just a process—it had become a way of life with billions in rated business.

In the weeks that followed, the lawns signs were pulled up, the attack ads stopped, and the pundits moved on to the next controversy. But for the voters, there is no forgetting the craziness they'd just lived through. It lingered in conversations, in social media posts, and in the quiet tension that simmered just beneath the surface. The craziness of the American election cycle wasn't just a passing storm—it was now a permanent part of the landscape.

In the months following the election, the country experienced what could only be described as a

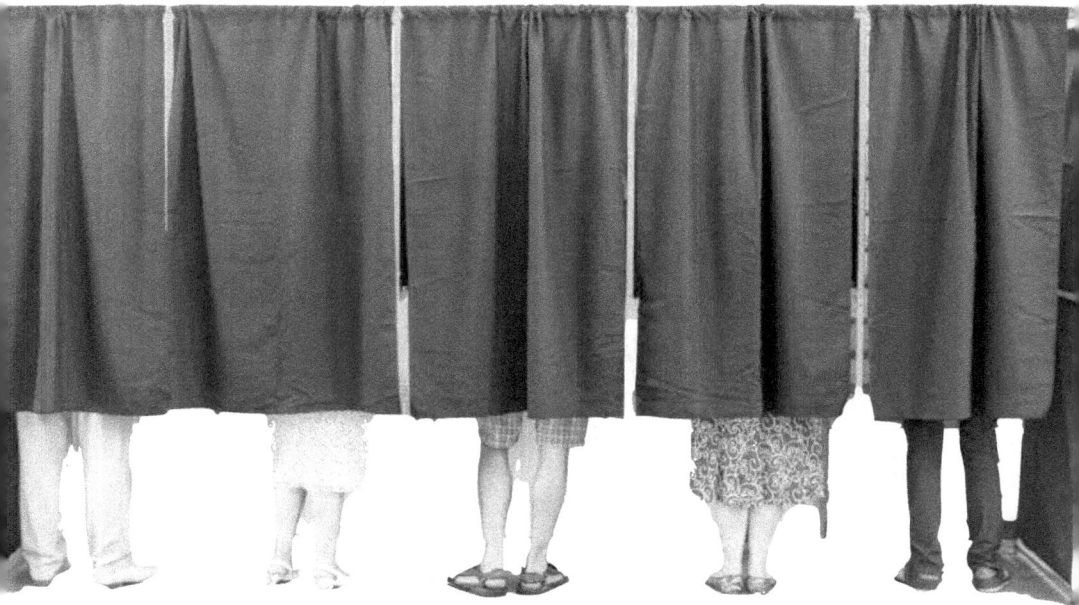

political hangover. For over a year, the election had been an all-consuming force, dominating headlines, conversations, and the national psyche. Then, seemingly overnight, it was over. The lawn signs were gone, the airwaves were free from attack ads, and the candidates' faces had all but disappeared from public view. Most folks thought 'Thank God!'

But the tension still lingers. Neighbors who had argued about politics didn't suddenly become friends again. Family members who'd unfollowed each other on Facebook weren't rushing to reconnect. The divisions stoked during the campaign still burned hot, even if the flames had subsided.

In Washington, the newly elected officials took their oaths of office, but even their sense of victory was muted. Governing after such a divisive election is always difficult, but now it felt almost impossible. The rhetoric of the campaign had set expectations so high that anything less than sweeping, immediate change was bound to disappoint. The reality, as

always, was that change in America came slowly, if at all. There's too much money at stake. And in fact most experts agree that the number one hurdle to campaign and election reform in America is the National Association of Broadcasters. Each cycle radio and TV broadcasters rake in billions in political ads. The more than 15,000 radio and 7500 TV broadcasters across the USA are fully vested in things not changing and lobby for the status quo.

Meanwhile, the losing side simmered with resentment. Conspiracy theories about voter fraud and election interference flourished, fueled by social media and partisan news outlets. The anger didn't fade; it festered, threatening to spill over into the streets. As the court cases get underway, for millions of Americans, the election isn't over—it had been stolen, rigged, or corrupted in some way. The truth didn't matter; what mattered was the feeling of betrayal. Our candidate didn't win.

One of the most disorienting aspects of the modern American election cycle is the way it amplifies the echo chambers people built for themselves. During the campaign, voters didn't just pick candidates— they picked entire worlds of information, where facts were tailored to their beliefs and reality was it was just a matter of opinion.

Social media platforms, with their algorithms designed to keep users engaged, had now become the primary source of news for millions of Americans. These platforms didn't just show people what was happening; they showed people what they wanted to see. It didn't matter if the information was accurate, so long as it confirmed their preexisting views. Tailored news!

The result was a nation living in multiple realities. For one side, the election had been a clear victory, a triumph of democracy. For the other, it was a stolen election, a fraud perpetrated by elites, the media and God knows what else. Each side had its own set of facts, its own experts, its own truths. There was no middle ground, no shared American reality to return to once the dust settled.

In this fractured landscape, dialogue was nearly impossible. Conversations about politics devolved into shouting matches or ended before they began. The idea of persuading someone from the "other side" seemed hopeless. Instead, people retreated further into their bubbles, surrounding themselves with like-minded individuals and filtering out any dissenting voices.

If there was one certainty in American politics, it was that the next campaign was always just around the corner. No sooner had the ballots been counted than the jockeying for the next election began. Politicians who had just won office were already thinking about their re-election campaigns. Strategists were crunching numbers, identifying swing states, and planning future strategies.

For political operatives, the election cycle never really end. The constant need for fundraising, the perpetual campaign mode, means there's never time to take a breath and focus solely on actually governing. Every decision made in Washington was scrutinized through the lens of its electoral consequences. Every vote was a potential campaign ad, every slip-up a future attack line.

The American public, weary from the previous 2016 and 2020 elections, could feel the gears of the next one already grinding into motion. There was a sense of inevitability about it, as though the country was trapped in a cycle it couldn't break free from. The craziness wasn't just a symptom of the system—it

was the system and 'performance politics' have become the normal… style over substance.

The role of the media in the American election cycle had always been central, but in recent years, it had taken on an almost surreal quality. Once upon a time, news outlets had been seen as arbiters of truth, institutions that provided the public with the information they needed to make informed decisions. But in the 24-hour news cycle, where ratings mattered more than facts, the media had become part of the madness and it still is.

Cable news channels, with their constant barrage of breaking news and punditry, treated every election as a crisis. Anchors breathlessly reported on every new poll, every minor gaffe, every campaign rally, as though the fate of the republic hung in the balance. It didn't matter that much of what they reported was noise; what mattered was keeping viewers glued to their screens.

Social media only made things worse. News was no longer consumed passively; it was engaged with, argued over, shared, and manipulated. Misinformation spread faster than facts, and by the time corrections were issued, it was too late. The damage had been done.

The result was a media landscape where the line between fact and fiction was blurred, where opinion masqueraded as news, and where the loudest voices drowned out everything else. In this environment, the craziness of the election cycle wasn't just tolerated—it was encouraged.

The American election cycle, for all its spectacle and drama, came at a cost. The constant campaigning, the divisiveness, the media frenzy—it all took a toll on the nation's psyche. Voter fatigue set in long before Election Day, leaving millions disillusioned and disconnected from the political process.

For many, the election cycle felt like a relentless onslaught, a never-ending series of conflicts and controversies that made it impossible to focus on anything else. The focus on personality over policy, on spectacle over substance, left voters feeling like they were part of a reality TV show, rather than a functioning democracy.

But the cost wasn't just psychological—it was financial, too. Billions of dollars are spent on campaigns, much of it going to media companies, consultants, and political operatives. The influence of money in politics had never been more apparent, with Super PACs and dark money groups flooding the airwaves with ads designed to sway voters.

The cost of running for office has become so astronomical that only the wealthiest or those with the backing of powerful interest groups can afford to compete. The result is a political system that feels increasingly out of reach for ordinary citizens, a system where money talks and voters are left wondering if their voices even mattered.

As the door closes on yet another exhausting election cycle, a question lingered in the air: is this really the best way to choose a leader? More and more Americans were beginning to question the sanity of the process, wondering if there was a better way to do democracy.

Reform movements sprang up, advocating for changes to the way elections were conducted. Proposals for ranked-choice voting, publicly funded campaigns, and shorter election cycles gained traction in some states. But for every call for change, there was resistance from those who benefited from the status quo.

Still, the discontent was palpable. Voters were tired —tired of the endless campaigning, tired of the

negative ads and tired of the media circus. They wanted something different, something better. But change, as always in American politics, was slow to come.

For now, the craziness of the election cycle seemed inescapable. But the seeds of change had been planted, and the question remained: how long could a nation survive under the weight of its own political insanity?

As the 2024 election fades into memory, the next election looms on the horizon, and with it, the promise of another round of chaos. The American election cycle is a machine that can't be stopped, a spectacle that can't be avoided. But even as the country braces for the next wave, there seems to be a growing sense that something has to give.

Whether that change would come in the form of electoral reform, media accountability, or a shift in the way campaigns are run, no one could say for sure. But one thing was certain: the craziness of the American election cycle isn't sustainable. Sooner or later, something will break.

In the meantime, the nation will continue to live in its political circus every four years watching as the show unfolds once again, hoping that this time, maybe things would be different.

CHAPTER 3

The DA
VP Kamala Harris Takes Center Stage

As the Democratic Party's presidential candidate, Kamala Harris stood at the intersection of several historic firsts. The daughter of immigrants, she was the first woman of African American and South Asian descent to serve as Vice President of the United States. Her rise in American politics is emblematic of a changing, increasingly diverse nation, and her candidacy in the 2024 election symbolizes a pivotal moment in both the Democratic Party and the nation's broader political landscape.

Harris brings a multifaceted background to her campaign: a career as a prosecutor, a U.S. Senator, and the first female Vice President. Her political identity has been shaped by a blend of pragmatism, ambition, and a deep commitment to justice reform and social equity. As the face of the Democratic ticket, Harris embodies the party's progressive yet moderate stance, aiming to unite the often-divergent wings of the Democratic base.

Kamala Devi Harris was born in Oakland, California, in 1964, to immigrant parents: Shyamala Gopalan, an Indian-American cancer researcher, and Donald Harris, a Jamaican-born economist. Harris' upbringing in Berkeley exposed her to the cultural and political movements of the time, shaping her worldview and inspiring her early interest in public service and the justice system.

Her mother, a central figure in Harris' life, instilled a sense of pride in both her Indian and African American heritage. Raised with a deep awareness of civil rights and social justice issues, Harris often cites her mother's influence as a driving force in her commitment to advocacy.

This personal narrative is integral to her political identity. Harris' candidacy represents not just her qualifications, but also a symbol of possibility for women and people of color. Her ability to navigate complex, intersecting identities has made her a powerful voice for a multicultural and evolving electorate.

Before entering the national political arena, Harris built a reputation as a tough, ambitious prosecutor in California. After graduating from Howard University and earning her law degree at the University of California, Hastings, Harris began her career as a deputy district attorney in Alameda County, focusing on prosecuting violent crimes.

In 2003, Harris made history when she was elected as the first Black woman to serve as the District Attorney of San Francisco. Her tenure was marked by both tough-on-crime policies and innovative reforms. She launched initiatives such as the Back on Track program, designed to reduce recidivism by providing job training and education to nonviolent offenders. However, her record as a prosecutor has not been without controversy. Critics have pointed to her handling of cases involving police misconduct and her reluctance to embrace progressive criminal

justice reforms during her early career. Still, Harris has consistently framed her prosecutorial background as an asset, arguing that it gives her a unique perspective on how to reform a justice system she worked within.

Harris took her prosecutorial style and tenacity to Washington, D.C. in 2017, becoming California's junior Senator. During her time in the Senate, she quickly gained a reputation for her sharp questioning during high-profile hearings, most notably those involving Supreme Court nominees and the Trump administration's cabinet officials. Her Senate career highlighted her focus on issues such as immigration reform, healthcare, and criminal justice. She co-sponsored the Medicare for All bill, signaling her alignment with progressive healthcare policies,

while also supporting legislation to provide more transparency in law enforcement and prison reform.

Harris' ability to balance the competing interests of the Democratic Party—appealing to both progressives and moderates—was seen as a key strength during her Senate career. Her policy positions were often pragmatic, aiming for incremental change that appealed to a broad spectrum of the electorate.

Kamala Harris made history again in 2020 when President Joe Biden selected her as his running mate, making her the first woman, the first Black woman, and the first person of South Asian descent to serve as Vice President. In this role, Harris took on significant responsibilities, including managing the administration's efforts on immigration, voting rights, and addressing the root causes of migration from Central America.

Harris' vice presidency, however, has been both a period of significant visibility and a challenge in finding clear-cut policy wins. The portfolio she was tasked with—especially on issues like the U.S.-Mexico border crisis—placed her in the midst of highly polarizing debates. Critics questioned the efficacy of her leadership in these areas, while supporters pointed out the systemic difficulties she faced in addressing long-standing issues.

Despite the challenges, Harris' historic presence in the White House has helped redefine the role of women in American politics. Her role as a barrier-breaker, coupled with her deft handling of diplomatic duties abroad, showcased her readiness for leadership on the global stage.

Harris' 2024 presidential campaign emphasizes positive themes of unity, progress, and inclusivity. Her platform seeks to build on the Biden administration's accomplishments while addressing issues that resonate deeply with the Democratic base and independents alike. Central to her campaign are policy proposals focused on economic recovery, healthcare expansion, climate change, and racial and social justice. There are four areas of focus for her;

• Economic Agenda: Harris advocates for economic reforms that prioritize working families, including expanded healthcare access, childcare support, and initiatives to close the racial wealth gap. She calls for a progressive tax system that ensures the wealthy pay their fair share.

• Criminal Justice Reform: Reflecting her evolution on justice issues, Harris' platform pushes for police reform, reducing mass incarceration, and decriminalizing marijuana. Her stance reflects a commitment to transforming the criminal justice system in ways that protect communities while promoting fairness.

•Climate Action: Harris has been vocal about her commitment to combating climate change, advocating for aggressive green energy policies, investment in sustainable infrastructure, and job creation through clean energy initiatives.

• Voting Rights and Democracy: Harris champions the protection of voting rights, supporting legislation to expand access to the ballot and counter state-level restrictions that disproportionately affect minorities and young voters.

Despite her historic candidacy, Harris faced significant challenges in the 2024 race. Public

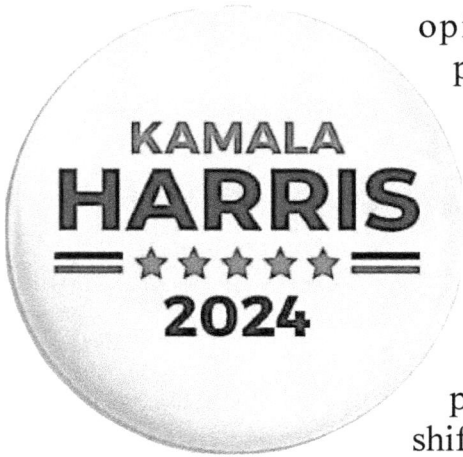

opinion has often been polarized, with some Democrats questioning her ability to appeal to moderate and rural voters, while Republicans have targeted her as a symbol of the Democratic Party's perceived radical leftward shift, real or imagined.

Harris has often been criticized for her handling of key issues, her perceived distance from the public. Her opponents have frequently labeled her as too liberal for middle America, while some progressives argue she is not liberal enough on key issues like healthcare reform and student debt cancellation. Election watchers are aware of the balancing act. As a candidate, Harris needed to navigate the delicate balance between appealing to the party's progressive base while also reaching out to moderates and independent voters—a balancing act tour de force.

Kamala Harris represents both continuity and change within the Democratic Party. As the first woman of color to run for the presidency on a major party ticket, her candidacy embodies the diversity and progress of America's future. Her career, marked by achievements and challenges, positions her as a compelling figure for voters seeking a leader who understands the complexities of both justice and governance.

In 2024, Harris was not just running as a continuation of the Biden administration but as a candidate who promises to forge a new path forward —one that addresses the deep-seated issues of inequality, climate change, and economic disparity while uniting a divided country. Whether she can succeed in transforming her historic presence into political victory remains to be seen, but there's no doubt that Kamala Harris has already changed the face of American politics… forever.

CHAPTER 4

Trump… Redux
The Former and Next President?

It was an unprecedented return. Donald Trump, the 2024 Republican presidential candidate, a figure who has redefined modern American politics, was back. After serving one tumultuous term as president, Trump remains one of the most polarizing yet influential figures in U.S. political history. His return to the presidential campaign, after losing the 2020 election, is unprecedented in the modern era. A billionaire businessman turned reality TV star, and later, an unconventional president, Trump's candidacy for a second term represents both a continuation of his populist vision and a deepening of the divisions that have come to define American politics since his first run in 2016.

Donald John Trump was born in 1946 in Queens, New York, into a wealthy family. His father, Fred Trump, was a real estate developer, and young Donald quickly followed in his footsteps. By the 1980s, Trump had become a major figure in the world of real estate, developing iconic properties like Trump Tower in Manhattan. Alongside his business ventures, Trump crafted an image as a larger-than-life figure—an image that would serve him well when he transitioned to politics. And while that might be effective at a campaign rally it remained to be seen if it was in the Oval Office.

The Trump brand is a real and perceived advantage. Trump mastered the art of self-promotion early in his real estate career, becoming synonymous with wealth, luxury, and success. His ventures included hotels, casinos, and golf courses, but also a string of bankruptcies and lawsuits that shaped his controversial business career. Trump's role as the star of the reality TV show 'The Apprentice' from 2004 to 2015 catapulted him to a new level of fame. The show presented Trump as a decisive, no-nonsense leader and businessman, and his famous catchphrase, "You're fired!" became emblematic of his image as a tough decision-maker.

By the time Trump announced his GOP candidacy for the presidency in 2015, he had built a powerful personal brand that blended business acumen, celebrity, and a willingness to challenge the political establishment. It was this blend of characteristics that made him a formidable—and controversial—political candidate.

The 2016 Campaign was designed to be a populist revolution and Trump's was unlike anything American politics had ever seen. Entering a crowded Republican primary field, Trump distinguished himself by rejecting the traditional norms of political discourse. His blunt rhetoric, willingness to attack both Republicans and Democrats, and his ability to connect with disaffected voters quickly propelled him to the top of the GOP race. His populist appeal was undeniable. Trump's campaign focused on issues like immigration, trade, and

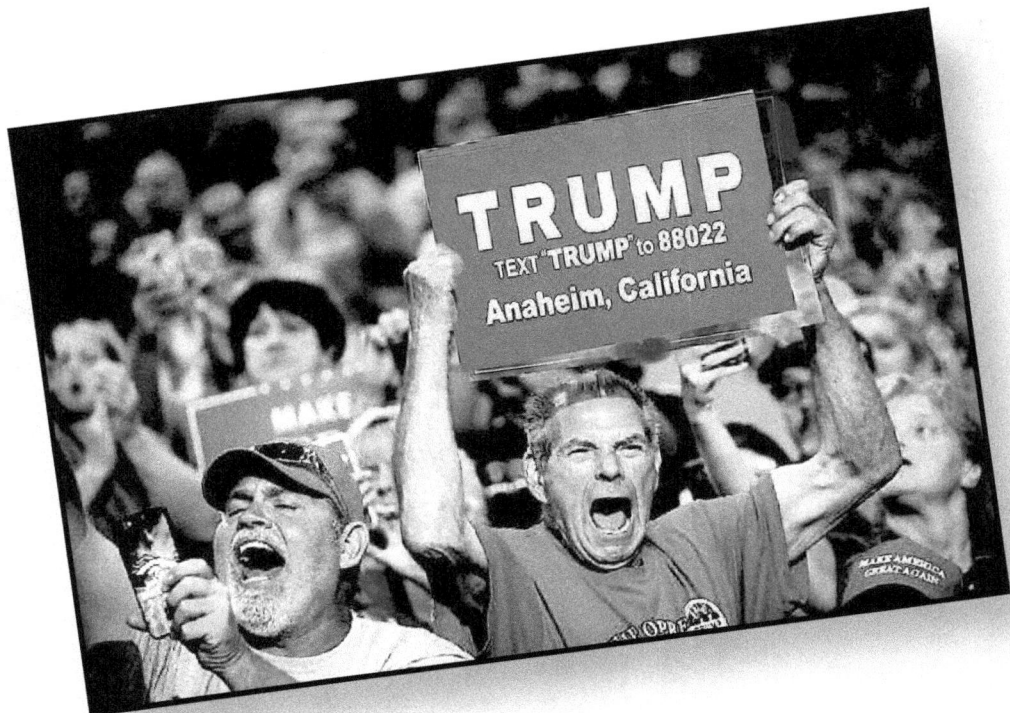

"draining the DC swamp" of political corruption. His promise to build a wall on the U.S.-Mexico border and his 'America-first' approach to trade resonated with white working-class voters who felt left behind by globalization and elite politics. He established himself as the Anti-Establishment Candidate, positioning himself as an outsider, running against not just the Democrats but the Republican establishment and career politicians as well. His disdain for traditional political decorum, paired with his attacks on media outlets, created a fervent base of supporters who saw him as a champion of the people and a God appointed savior.

His victory shocked political pundits and marked the beginning of a new, hyper-polarized era in American politics. Trump's 2016 campaign established the key elements of his political persona: a rejection of political correctness, a direct appeal to voter frustration, and a willingness to exploit cultural and economic anxieties. This approach laid the foundation for his presidency and the movement that continued to drive his political ambitions in 2024 and possibility into the future. One thing is certain Donald Trump's presidency from 2017 to 2021 was marked by controversy, upheaval, and an unrelenting focus on his brand of populist politics. From day one, Trump sought to challenge the norms of Washington, embracing chaos as a political strategy and disrupting both domestic and international policies.

Foremost among these was Immigration policy and the Border Wall. Trump's hardline stance on immigration was central to his presidency. His administration implemented a series of controversial policies, including the travel ban targeting predominantly Muslim countries and the "zero tolerance" policy that resulted in family separations at the U.S.-Mexico border. The border wall, though not completed as promised, remained a symbol of his commitment to controlling immigration.

On economic policy, tax cuts and deregulation were the goals. Trump's economic policy focused on cutting taxes and rolling back regulations. The 2017 Tax Cuts and Jobs Act was the signature legislative

58

achievement of his presidency, providing significant tax relief to corporations and wealthy individuals. Trump also pursued an aggressive deregulatory agenda, particularly in environmental and financial sectors. His Foreign Policy was simple... 'America First!' In foreign policy, Trump upended traditional alliances and embraced a unilateralist approach. He withdrew the U.S. from several international agreements, including the Paris Climate Accord and the Iran nuclear deal and also engaged in high-profile diplomacy with North Korea. His meeting with Kim Jong-un in an unprecedented summit, while colorful failed to produce any lasting results.

For the first time in American history, Trump's presidency was marked by two impeachments—first for his efforts to pressure Ukraine into investigating President Joe Biden, and later for his role in the January 6th Capitol insurrection. These scandals, along with ongoing investigations into his financial dealings, kept Trump at the center of controversy throughout his 2016 term. Despite the constant turbulence, Trump maintained an intensely loyal base of supporters who saw his presidency as a necessary corrective to what they viewed as the failures of the political establishment. He was defined as much by the battles fought with political opponents as by the policies he implemented.

The 2020 election and its aftermath—with Trump's refusal to concede was a watershed moment. The election saw Donald Trump face off against Joe Biden in one of the most contentious and high-

stakes elections in U.S. history. Amidst the COVID pandemic, Trump's handling of the crisis became a central issue, as did the broader cultural and political divisions that had defined his presidency. Despite securing over 74 million votes, the highest total for a sitting president, Trump lost the Electoral College and popular vote to Biden. His refusal to accept the results led to baseless claims of widespread voter fraud and led to his efforts to overturn the election outcome. Trump's persistent claims of a stolen election culminated in the January 6th, 2021, attack on the U.S. Capitol where his supporters at his encouragement sought to disrupt the certification of Biden's victory. Trump's role in inciting the insurrection led to his second impeachment, though he was narrowly acquitted in the Senate. The events of January 6th fractured the country even deeper and the post insurrection reshaped the GOP, with Trump's influence continuing to dominate the party even after his departure from office. His refusal to concede the election and the ensuing chaos left a lasting legacy of division and mistrust in the electoral process which was something new.

From the start Donald Trump's 2024 presidential campaign was an unprecedented return to national politics. While many believed his defeat in 2020 and the fallout from January 6th might end his political career, Trump has instead doubled down on his core message of populism and grievance politics. Nicknamed but some in the his circle the "Campaign of Retribution" Trump's 2024 campaign was driven by a desire to reclaim power and settle scores. He continued to frame himself as a victim of a corrupt political establishment, amplifying claims of

election fraud from 2020 and vowing to dismantle what he calls the "deep state."

Support from the GOP base continued to be substantial despite the controversies surrounding his presidency and post-presidency actions. Even today Trump remains the dominant figure in the Republican Party. His base of supporters are as energized as ever. 2024 had Trump pledge to continue the policies of his first term, with a focus on immigration, economic nationalism, and deregulation. He had also hinted at further radical reforms to government institutions, including purging the civil service and consolidating executive power. Trump's return to the political arena forced the Republican Party to reckon with its identity and future. For many in the GOP, Trump's brand of populism and combative style is the only path forward, while others worry about the long-term consequences of his divisive leadership. With the outcome of the 2024 election, Donald Trump's influence on American politics will endure. His brand of populism, characterized by nationalism, anti-elitism, and a willingness to break political norms, has reshaped not only the Republican Party but the broader US political landscape as well.

The candidate and his supporters made it clear that this was a movement and not just one candidate. MAGAism is more than just Donald Trump—it's a political movement that has redefined conservative politics in the U.S. Its emphasis on anti-globalism, economic protectionism, and cultural conservatism has energized a base that feels alienated by both the Democratic Party and establishment Republicans. Trump's political style has deepened the partisan divide in our country, with his supporters viewing him as a savior of traditional American values. His detractors seeing him as a threat to democratic institutions. The polarization will likely persist.

Donald Trump's influence on American politics, and the Republican Party in particular, is likely to endure

long after the 2024 election. His rise to power marked the beginning of a new era of populism and political disruption, reshaping the way candidates campaign, how the media covers politics, and how voters engage with their leaders. Trump has fundamentally altered the Republican Party, turning it into a vehicle for his personal brand of nationalism, anti-establishment rhetoric, and populist fervor. The movement he has cultivated—dubbed "Trumpism"—will continue to shape the future of American conservatism. GOP candidates running for office, both at the local and national levels, will be measured against Trump's image, with his base demanding loyalty to his vision and ideals. His ability to galvanize voters with a blend of economic nationalism, fear of cultural change, and disdain for political correctness has created a template for future Republican leaders.

But Trump's legacy also carries significant risks. The deepening of political polarization, the erosion of trust in democratic institutions, and the normalization of inflammatory, divisive rhetoric have left the country more divided than ever. His refusal to accept the results of legitimate elections, and his guilt in the January 6th Capitol riot, has exposed vulnerabilities in the electoral process and raised concerns about the future of traditional American democracy.

In the broader scope of history, Trump will likely be remembered as a transformative, controversial figure—one whose rise to power both reflected and fueled the frustrations of a large segment of the American electorate. His enduring popularity among his base and his outsized influence over the Republican Party suggest that Trumpism is not a passing phase, but a force that will shape the political landscape for years to come.

Ultimately, Trump's 2024 campaign was not just about winning back the presidency—it was about solidifying his place in history as a leader who challenged the status quo and reshaped the political order in his own image. Whether that legacy will be viewed as a triumph or a cautionary tale remains to be seen. But one thing is certain: Donald Trump has left an indelible mark on American politics that will not be easily erased.

CHAPTER 5

MONEY & POLITICS

The Currency of Influence

Money has always been a powerful force in U.S. politics, but in the 21st century, its influence has reached unprecedented levels. Campaigns, advocacy groups, and political parties spend billions of dollars every election cycle, funneling resources into ads, outreach, and voter mobilization efforts. But beyond the dollar amounts lies a deeper question: what does this influx of money mean for American democracy?

In many ways, the story of money in politics is the story of access and influence. Those who can contribute large sums often have greater sway over policy decisions, while those without the financial means may struggle to have their voices heard. This has sparked widespread concerns about the role of money in corrupting the democratic process and distorting policy outcomes in favor of the wealthy and powerful.

At the same time, advocates of deregulated campaign finance argue that political donations are a form of free speech, protected by the First Amendment. The debate over how to regulate money in politics has divided policymakers, activists, and courts for decades, with landmark decisions like Citizens United v. FEC reshaping the landscape of political spending.

This book seeks to explore the complex and often controversial relationship between money and politics in the United States. From the historical evolution of campaign finance laws to the rise of dark money and Super PACs, we will examine how money flows through the political system and its impact on governance, accountability, and the future of American democracy.

The influence of money in U.S. politics is nothing new. Since the earliest days of the republic, candidates have sought financial support to fund their campaigns and secure electoral victories. In the 19th century, political machines often used patronage and kickbacks to maintain control over local and state elections. Wealthy industrialists, like the infamous Gilded Age robber barons, frequently bankrolled politicians to ensure favorable policies for their businesses.

The first serious attempts to regulate money in politics began in the early 20th century during the Progressive Era. Reformers, concerned about the undue influence of corporations and special interests, pushed for greater transparency and limits on campaign contributions. The Tillman Act of 1907 was the first federal law to ban corporate contributions to federal candidates. However, enforcement was weak, and money continued to play a major role in elections.

The Watergate scandal in the 1970s exposed the extent to which illegal campaign contributions had been used to influence President Nixon's re-election campaign. In response, Congress passed the Federal Election Campaign Act (FECA) of 1974, which established limits on individual contributions, required campaigns to disclose their donors, and created the Federal Election Commission (FEC) to enforce the new rules.

These reforms represented a significant step forward in regulating money in politics, but they also sowed the seeds for future conflicts over campaign finance.

Loopholes in the law, coupled with court decisions that expanded the definition of political speech, opened the door for new forms of spending to flood the system.

In the wake of the Watergate reforms, Political Action Committees (PACs) emerged as a new way for interest groups to influence elections. PACs allowed corporations, unions, and other organizations to pool money from donors and direct it toward political campaigns, subject to contribution limits. These committees became a powerful force in U.S. elections, giving businesses and labor unions a way to support candidates who aligned with their interests.

By the 1980s and 1990s, political parties had begun to exploit loopholes in campaign finance law to raise "soft money," funds that were not subject to federal limits because they were supposedly intended for party-building activities rather than direct campaign support. In practice, soft money was often used to fund issue ads and other activities that directly benefited candidates, effectively circumventing contribution limits.

The Bipartisan Campaign Reform Act (BCRA): Known as the McCain-Feingold Act, the BCRA of 2002 sought to address the growing influence of soft money in elections. The law banned the use of soft money by political parties and placed new restrictions on issue ads funded by outside groups. It also raised the limits on individual contributions to campaigns, adjusting for inflation.

While the BCRA was a landmark piece of legislation, it was far from the final word on campaign finance. In fact, just a few years after its passage, the law would be dramatically weakened by a series of court rulings that expanded the rights of corporations and wealthy individuals to spend unlimited amounts on elections.

In 2010, the Supreme Court issued one of the most consequential decisions in the history of campaign finance law: Citizens United v. Federal Election Commission. The case revolved around a conservative nonprofit organization, Citizens United, which had produced a documentary critical of then-Senator Hillary Clinton. The FEC argued that the documentary violated campaign finance rules, but the Supreme Court disagreed, ruling in a 5-4 decision that restrictions on independent political spending by corporations and unions violated the First Amendment's protection of free speech. These decisions are still being debated.

The Impact of the decision was profound! The Citizens United decision opened the floodgates for unlimited political spending by corporations, unions, and wealthy individuals. The Court reasoned that as long as the spending was independent of a candidate's campaign, it could not be restricted. This led to the creation of Super PACs—independent expenditure-only committees that can raise and spend unlimited amounts of money to influence elections.

Super PACs quickly became a dominant force in U.S. elections, allowing wealthy donors to exert significant influence over campaigns. While Super PACs are technically prohibited from coordinating directly with candidates, in practice, the lines between campaigns and Super PACs are often blurred. Many Super PACs are run by close associates of the candidates they support, and their ads frequently promote the same messages as the candidates themselves.

The rise of Super PACs has led to a dramatic increase in the cost of running for office, particularly at the federal level. Presidential campaigns now routinely cost billions of dollars, with candidates relying heavily on outside groups to fund the massive advertising blitzes needed to sway voters.
While Super PACs are required to disclose their donors, another category of political spending has emerged that allows donors to remain anonymous with 'dark money'. Dark money refers to political spending by nonprofit organizations—such as

501(c)(4) social welfare groups and 501(c)(6) trade associations—that are not required to disclose their donors. These groups can spend money on political activities, including issue ads that influence elections, without revealing their funding sources.

Dark money groups have become a key player in U.S. elections, particularly in swing states and competitive congressional races. Because they do not have to disclose their donors, these groups allow wealthy individuals and corporations to influence elections without accountability. Dark money has been used to fund everything from attack ads against candidates to grassroots lobbying efforts aimed at swaying public opinion.

The rise of dark money is largely the result of legal loopholes that allow certain types of nonprofit organizations to engage in political activities without being subject to the same disclosure requirements as PACs or Super PACs. While these nonprofits are technically supposed to focus on social welfare activities, the line between issue advocacy and electioneering is often thin. As a

73

result, many dark money groups spend the majority of their budgets on political activities, even as they claim to be focused on nonpartisan causes.

While campaign contributions and political spending are the most visible ways that money influences U.S. politics, they are far from the only methods. Lobbying—the act of attempting to influence lawmakers and government officials—has long been a major industry in Washington, D.C., with businesses, trade associations, unions, and advocacy groups spending billions of dollars each year to shape policy decisions. Lobbying firms are often staffed by former lawmakers, political staffers, and government officials who use their insider knowledge and connections to advocate on behalf of their clients. These clients can range from Fortune 500 companies to environmental groups, all of whom seek to influence legislation, regulations, and government contracts.

The influence of lobbyists on policy can be profound. Lobbyists often help draft legislation, provide lawmakers with research and talking points, and even organize public campaigns to generate support for their clients' positions. This has raised concerns about the extent to which policymaking is driven by special interests rather than the public good. One of the most controversial aspects of lobbying is the "revolving door," the practice of government officials leaving public service to work for lobbying firms or private companies they once regulated. This creates potential conflicts of interest,

as former officials may use their connections and influence to benefit their new employers.

The 2024 presidential election was the most expensive in U.S. history, with more than $14 billion spent by candidates, parties, PACs, and outside groups. The sheer scale of spending underscored the extent to which money now dominates American politics. Both major party candidates, Joe Biden and Donald Trump, raised unprecedented sums of money. Much of the spending was in battleground states; Pennsylvania, Michigan, and Georgia.

Super PACs played a significant role both in the 2020 and '24 election, with outside groups spending heavily to support or oppose candidates. Billionaire donors on both sides of the political spectrum contributed millions to these groups, ensuring that their preferred candidates could flood the airwaves with ads and outspend their opponents. While Super

PACs are required to operate independently from campaigns, their influence was palpable, particularly in swing states where they launched targeted ad campaigns to sway undecided voters.

The use of dark money also increased in 2020, as politically active nonprofits spent hundreds of millions of dollars on the election. These groups operated under the radar, with little public accountability, and helped shape the narrative around key issues such as healthcare, immigration, and the economy. Dark money groups were particularly active in Senate races, where they funneled undisclosed funds into tight contests that could determine the balance of power in Congress.

While big money from wealthy donors and corporations dominated much of the campaign finance landscape, the 2020 election also saw an explosion of small-dollar donations. Fueled by online fundraising platforms like ActBlue and WinRed, both the Biden and Trump campaigns raised substantial amounts of money from grassroots supporters who contributed in increments of $200 or less. This surge in small donations helped offset some of the influence of large donors and demonstrated the power of digital fundraising in modern politics.

The outsized role of money in U.S. politics has raised serious concerns about the health of democracy. Critics argue that the influence of wealthy donors and special interests distorts policy outcomes, undermines public trust, and limits the ability of ordinary citizens to participate meaningfully in the political process. One of the most significant consequences of big money in politics is the risk of policy capture—when government decisions are disproportionately shaped by the interests of a small, wealthy elite. Whether it's tax policy, healthcare reform, or environmental regulation, there is evidence that lawmakers often prioritize the concerns of major donors over those of their constituents. This has led to a growing sense of disillusionment among voters, who feel that the political system is rigged in favor of the rich.

The perception that money corrupts the political process has contributed to a widespread decline in public trust in government. Polls consistently show that Americans believe politicians are more responsive to the needs of big donors than to the needs of ordinary citizens. This erosion of trust has dangerous implications for democracy, as it fuels cynicism, disengagement, and a belief that the political system is incapable of addressing the real problems facing the country.

The skyrocketing cost of running for office has made it increasingly difficult for candidates without access to wealthy donors to compete. This has created a barrier to entry for many would-be candidates, particularly those from underrepresented communities who may not have the financial networks needed to mount a successful campaign. As a result, the pool of candidates has become less diverse, both in terms of race and class, limiting the range of perspectives represented in government. Despite the challenges posed by the influence of money in politics, there have been numerous efforts over the years to reform the campaign finance system. From legislative proposals to grassroots movements, activists and lawmakers have sought to limit the power of big money and increase transparency and accountability in political spending.

One of the most ambitious reform ideas is the public financing of elections. Under this system, candidates would receive government funding to run their campaigns, reducing their reliance on private donors. Several states and cities, including Maine and New York City, have implemented public financing programs with varying degrees of success. Advocates argue that public financing would level the playing field, allowing candidates to compete based on the strength of their ideas rather than the size of their war chests. Increasing transparency in political spending is another key area of reform. Proposals such as the DISCLOSE Act aim to require dark money groups to disclose their donors, making it more difficult for anonymous donors to influence elections without public accountability. While efforts to pass federal disclosure laws have stalled in Congress, some states have taken action to increase transparency at the state and local levels.

Another avenue of reform involves limiting the influence of corporations and foreign entities in U.S.

Courtesy New York Times

elections. While corporate donations to candidates are still banned under the Tillman Act, Citizens United allows corporations to spend unlimited amounts on independent expenditures. Some reformers have called for a constitutional amendment to overturn Citizens United, though such efforts face significant political and legal hurdles. Additionally, there is growing concern about the role of foreign money in U.S. elections, particularly in the wake of revelations about Russian interference in the 2016 presidential race.

The digital age has transformed the way money flows through politics. Advances in technology have made it easier for candidates to raise funds from small donors, but they have also enabled new forms of political spending that are harder to regulate.

Platforms like 'ActBlue' and 'WinRed' have revolutionized grassroots fundraising, allowing campaigns to raise millions of dollars from small donors with the click of a button. These platforms have democratized political giving, enabling more people to participate in the process. However, they have also raised questions about the transparency of online donations, particularly when it comes to foreign money or donations made through untraceable digital currencies like Bitcoin.

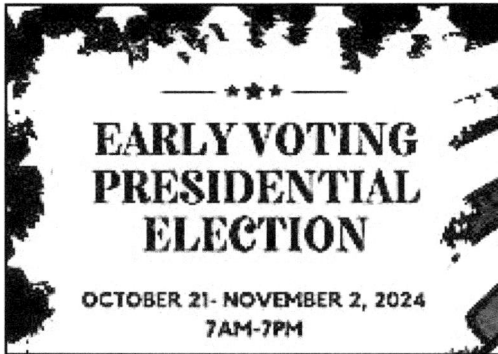

Social media platforms like Facebook and Twitter have become essential tools for political campaigns, allowing them to reach voters with highly targeted ads based on demographic and behavioral data. While micro-targeting can be an effective way to mobilize supporters, it has also raised concerns about privacy, misinformation, and the ability of

outside groups to influence elections with little oversight. In recent years, there have been calls for greater regulation of political advertising on social media, particularly when it comes to disclosing who is behind the ads and how they are being funded.

Campaigns now have access to vast amounts of data on voters, allowing them to craft highly personalized messages and optimize their spending for maximum impact. This data-driven approach to campaigning has been credited with helping candidates like President Barack Obama and Donald Trump win their elections, but it has also raised ethical concerns about the use of personal data for political purposes. The increasing reliance on data analytics has made elections more expensive and further entrenched the role of big money in politics, as campaigns invest heavily in technology and expertise to gain a competitive edge.

The influence of money in U.S. politics has reached a critical juncture. As campaigns grow ever more expensive, and the role of dark money and Super PACs continues to expand, the question remains: can American democracy survive the dominance of big money? The concentration of political power in the hands of a few wealthy donors threatens the very foundations of democracy. When a small elite can determine the outcome of elections and shape policy to suit their interests, the principles of equality and representation are undermined. This creates a system in which the voices of ordinary citizens are drowned out, and the gap between the governed and their representatives widens.

Despite the challenges, there is reason for hope. Grassroots movements advocating for campaign finance reform have gained momentum in recent years, and public support for limiting the influence of money in politics remains strong. Efforts to implement public financing, increase transparency, and regulate digital spending offer potential solutions to the problems posed by big money. Ultimately, the future of campaign finance reform will depend on the political will of lawmakers and the engagement of the public. If voters demand change and hold their elected officials accountable, there is a chance to create a more equitable and transparent political system—one in which money plays a less dominant role, and the voices of ordinary citizens are heard.

The intersection of money and politics has long shaped the trajectory of U.S. governance, often skewing power toward those with financial resources. While reforms have been attempted and public pressure continues to build, the future of campaign finance remains uncertain. Whether democracy can withstand the corrosive influence of money will depend on the strength of political will and our institutions. The demand for accountability from the American people will continue.

Chapter 6

Trump's Victory
A Historic and Polarizing Win!

The 2024 U.S. presidential election will go down in history as one of the most contentious and closely watched elections in modern American history. Against all odds, former President Donald Trump secured a second, non-consecutive term, a feat only achieved once before in U.S. history by Grover Cleveland. Trump's return to the White House symbolized not just a resurgence of his personal political brand, but also a larger movement within American politics—one that rejected establishment norms, embraced populist rhetoric, and underscored the deep divisions within the country. This victory, although hard-fought and controversial, was a result of various factors converging at a critical moment in the nation's history.

Donald Trump's decision to run for president in 2024 was met with both anticipation and skepticism. After losing the 2020 election to Joe Biden, Trump remained a dominant force within the Republican Party, despite his numerous legal troubles, including multiple indictments related to the January 6th Capitol riot and ongoing investigations into his business dealings. Many political analysts predicted that these challenges would prevent Trump from mounting a successful campaign. However, Trump's loyal base of supporters, combined with his relentless determination to dominate the political narrative, ensured that he would once again be a major player on the national stage.

The Republican primary leading up to the 2024 election was fiercely contested, with several prominent figures vying for the nomination. Florida Governor Ron DeSantis, South Carolina Senator Tim Scott, and former Secretary of State Mike Pompeo were among the leading contenders. Yet, despite the strong competition, Trump's ability to galvanize his base and frame himself as the only true outsider candidate set him apart. His strategy of using rallies, social media, and right-wing news outlets to communicate directly with his supporters allowed him to bypass traditional media and maintain his hold on the party.

Trump's message during the primaries was a continuation of his "America First" platform from his previous campaigns. He railed against globalism, criticized the Biden administration's handling of the economy and foreign policy, and promised to restore what he called "American greatness." His attacks on political correctness, cancel culture, and the mainstream media resonated deeply with a significant portion of the electorate, particularly in rural areas and among white working-class voters who felt left behind by the Democratic Party.

As the primary season progressed, Trump's opponents struggled to differentiate themselves from him without alienating his base. While some candidates attempted to position themselves as more moderate or forward-looking alternatives to Trump, they ultimately failed to gain traction. Trump's dominance in the Republican Party was solidified when he secured key endorsements from influential conservative figures, including several members of Congress and popular media personalities like Sean Hannity and Tucker Carlson.

By the time the Republican National Convention arrived, it was clear that Trump was the overwhelming favorite. Despite some dissent within the party's establishment wing, the Republican base rallied behind Trump with fervor. His acceptance speech at the convention was a fiery rebuke of the political establishment, filled with populist rhetoric and promises to restore law and order, strengthen the economy, and put American interests first on the world stage. Trump's nomination set the stage for what would be a bruising general election campaign.

On the Democratic side, Vice President Kamala Harris emerged as the party's nominee after a challenging primary season of her own. President Joe Biden, after much speculation, announced that he would not seek a second term, citing his age and the need for new leadership within the Democratic Party. Harris, having served as vice president for four years, positioned herself as the logical successor to Biden's legacy, emphasizing continuity in areas like healthcare, climate change, and justice.

However, Harris's path to the nomination was not without obstacles. She faced stiff competition from progressive challengers like Senator Bernie Sanders and Representative Alexandria Ocasio-Cortez, who criticized her for being too centrist and not doing enough to address income inequality, student debt, and systemic racism. Additionally, moderate Democrats like Senator Amy Klobuchar and Governor Gavin Newsom argued that Harris's progressive policies would alienate swing voters in key battleground states. They did.

Despite the internal divisions within the Democratic Party, Harris ultimately secured the nomination after a series of high-profile endorsements from party leaders, including Barack Obama and Hillary Clinton. Her campaign sought to build a broad coalition of voters, including women, people of color, young voters, and suburban moderates who had been instrumental in Biden's 2020 victory. Harris emphasized the need to protect democracy, combat climate change, and expand healthcare access, framing her campaign as a continuation of Biden's policies while also addressing the unique challenges of a post-pandemic world.

The general election quickly became a referendum on Trump's previous presidency and the direction of the country. For many Democratic voters, a second Trump term represented a threat to the core values of democracy and decency, while Trump's supporters saw Harris as a continuation of what they felt were the failures of President Biden.

One of the central issues of the 2024 election was the state of the economy. By the time the election campaign was in full swing, the U.S. economy was grappling with persistent inflation, rising interest rates, and stagnant wage growth. Although the Biden administration had overseen a robust economic recovery following the COVID-19 pandemic, the lingering effects of inflation and supply chain disruptions had eroded much of that progress. Voters were concerned about the rising cost of living, particularly in housing, healthcare, and energy.

Trump seized on these economic concerns, framing himself as the only candidate capable of restoring prosperity. He frequently pointed to his economic record during his first term, which included tax cuts, deregulation, and historically low unemployment rates prior to the pandemic. Trump's message was clear: the Biden administration had mismanaged the economy, and only he could fix it. His economic platform focused on cutting taxes, reducing government spending, and bringing manufacturing jobs back through protectionist trade policies.

In contrast, Harris's campaign emphasized the need for continued investment in infrastructure, clean energy, and social programs. She argued that the economic challenges facing the country required long-term solutions that addressed inequality and promoted sustainable growth. Harris also criticized Trump's tax cuts for the wealthy and corporations, vowing to raise taxes on the rich to fund expanded healthcare and education programs.

Despite Harris's efforts to shift the conversation toward progressive economic policies, Trump's simple and direct messaging on inflation and jobs resonated with voters who were struggling to make ends meet. His promise to cut gas prices, lower taxes, and bring back manufacturing jobs played particularly well in swing states like Michigan, Pennsylvania, and Wisconsin, where voters had been hit hard by economic uncertainty.

Immigration and border security were once again central themes in the 2024 election, particularly as the southern border continued to experience high levels of migrant crossings. Trump, who had made immigration a cornerstone of his 2016 campaign, returned to the issue with a vengeance in 2024. He doubled down on his promise to complete the border wall and implement stricter immigration policies, including ending birthright citizenship and increasing deportations.

For Trump's base, immigration represented a clear and present danger to the country's security and cultural identity. His rhetoric on the campaign trail often invoked fears of crime, drug trafficking, and economic competition from undocumented workers.

Trump's hardline stance on immigration, combined with his ability to tie the issue to broader concerns about national sovereignty and law and order, helped him energize his supporters.

Harris, on the other hand, took a more measured approach to immigration. As a former prosecutor and vice president, she advocated for comprehensive immigration reform that included a path to citizenship for undocumented immigrants, protections for Dreamers, and increased funding for border security technology. Harris framed immigration as a humanitarian issue, arguing that the U.S. needed to address the root causes of migration, like violence and poverty.

However, Harris's position on immigration faced criticism from both the left and the right. Progressives argued that her policies were not bold enough, while conservatives attacked her for being too lenient on border security. Trump capitalized on this perceived weakness, portraying Harris as a proponent of "open borders" and accusing her of prioritizing the needs of immigrants over those of American citizens.

The immigration debate played a particularly important role in key battleground states like Arizona and Texas, where voters were deeply divided on the issue. In these states, Trump's tough-on-immigration message helped him win over suburban and rural voters who were concerned about border security.

The issue of law and order was another defining feature of the 2024 election. In the years leading up to the election, the U.S. had experienced a series of high-profile incidents of social unrest, including protests against police brutality, violent clashes between far-right and far-left groups, and an increase in violent crime in some cities. These issues became a flashpoint in the campaign, with both candidates offering starkly different visions of how to address them.

Trump, as he had in 2020, positioned himself as the "law and order" candidate. He repeatedly condemned the Black Lives Matter movement, Antifa, and other progressive activists, accusing them of inciting violence and chaos in American cities. Trump's campaign ads frequently featured images of burning buildings, looted stores, and clashes between protesters and police the message being that only he can restore peace and security.

Harris, in contrast, acknowledged the need for police reform and the importance of addressing systemic racism, but she also sought to distance herself from the more radical elements of the progressive movement. She called for common-sense reforms to policing, such as increased accountability, improved training, and the establishment of national standards for use of force. At the same time, Harris emphasized her support for law enforcement and rejected calls from some progressives to defund the police, recognizing the importance of public safety, especially in communities of color that were often disproportionately affected by crime.

The law and order debate was a highly polarizing issue. Trump's base, especially in rural and suburban areas, resonated with his message of restoring order, feeling that their communities were under siege by urban unrest. Trump painted Harris as weak on crime and aligned her with the most radical elements of the Democratic Party, accusing her of supporting the "soft-on-crime" policies of cities like New York, Portland, and Chicago. His campaign successfully linked rising crime rates with what they described as Democratic governance failures, tapping into the fears of voters concerned about safety.

On the other hand, Harris tried to walk a fine line, acknowledging the legitimate concerns of both protestors and law enforcement. She advocated for policies aimed at reducing police violence while also ensuring that public safety remained a priority. However, her nuanced stance often struggled to break through in an election dominated by more extreme rhetoric from both sides. As violence in certain cities continued to make headlines, Trump's message of swift and decisive action seemed to gain more traction with undecided and swing voters.

In states like Wisconsin, Minnesota, and Pennsylvania—where both urban and suburban voters had a direct stake in the law and order debate —the issue became a significant factor in the final stretch of the campaign. Trump's calls for a return to "law and order" were seen as an answer to the perceived chaos, while Harris's message of reform and justice, though popular among younger and more diverse voters, had a harder time convincing older and more conservative-leaning voters.

The media landscape in 2024 was more fragmented and polarized than ever before. Traditional media outlets like CNN, MSNBC, and The New York Times continued to cover the election with a focus on fact-based reporting, but their reach had diminished among large swaths of the population, particularly Trump's supporters. Right-wing media outlets, such as Fox News, One America News Network (OANN), and Newsmax, played a pivotal role in shaping the narrative for Trump's base. These outlets provided a platform for Trump's message, often amplifying his claims of election fraud, his economic policies, and his attacks on Harris.

Social media, too, was a battleground for narratives, disinformation, and conspiracy theories. Trump's ability to dominate platforms like Facebook, X (formerly Twitter), and Truth Social, his own social media platform, allowed him to bypass traditional media filters and speak directly to his supporters. Despite his ban from certain mainstream platforms following the 2020 election, Trump remained highly visible on the internet, and alternative platforms that catered to conservative voices flourished during the campaign.

One of the most damaging aspects of the 2024 election was the continued spread of misinformation and disinformation, much of it centered around false claims of voter fraud. Trump had never fully conceded the results of the 2020 election, and his 2024 campaign was built, in part, on the promise to "fix" the electoral system. His rallies were filled with claims that the election system was rigged, particularly in Democratic-run cities and states, despite no substantial evidence supporting these claims. Right-wing media and social media networks perpetuated these narratives, making them a central theme of Trump's campaign.

Harris's campaign struggled to combat the spread of false information. While her team worked to correct disinformation and emphasize the importance of trusting the electoral process, the speed and scale at which conspiracy theories spread online made it difficult to keep up. Fact-checking organizations and mainstream news outlets frequently debunked Trump's claims, but for many of Trump's supporters, the media itself was seen as part of the problem, a sentiment Trump had spent years cultivating.

Harris did receive favorable coverage from liberal-leaning outlets like MSNBC and progressive online platforms, but these media ecosystems largely spoke to audiences who were already aligned with her politically. The polarization of media consumption meant that both candidates were, in many ways, preaching to their own choirs, making it difficult for either side to break through to undecided or swing voters.

Voter turnout in 2024 was expected to be high, much like the record-breaking turnout of 2020, but there were important demographic shifts that shaped the outcome of the election. Trump's path to victory relied on maintaining his dominance among white, working-class voters in the Midwest and expanding his support among Latino voters, particularly in states like Florida, Arizona, and Texas. Meanwhile, Harris sought to build a coalition that mirrored Biden's 2020 victory, with strong support from African Americans, young voters, suburban women, and college-educated whites.

However, some key dynamics had shifted since 2020. Trump had made surprising inroads with Latino voters in 2020, particularly in Florida and Texas, and he sought to expand this support in 2024. His message of economic opportunity, combined with his opposition to socialism and his hardline stance on law and order, resonated with more conservative Latino voters, especially Cuban Americans in Florida and Mexican Americans in the Rio Grande Valley. These voters, many of whom had been turned off by the Democratic Party's progressive wing, saw Trump as a defender of traditional values and economic freedom.

At the same time, Harris's campaign worked to mobilize African American and young voters, but turnout in these key demographics did not reach the

TIME

He Wins

historic levels seen in 2020. While Harris remained popular among these groups, her appeal did not generate the same level of enthusiasm that Biden had in 2020, particularly in key battleground states. The Democratic Party's failure to fully address issues like police reform and student debt alienated some younger voters and progressives, who saw Harris as too closely aligned with the establishment.

Suburban women, a key demographic that had swung toward Biden in 2020, were once again a battleground. While Trump had struggled with this group in his previous campaign due to his divisive rhetoric and handling of the COVID pandemic, his law-and-order message resonated with some suburban voters concerned about crime and safety. Harris's campaign worked to counter this by emphasizing her own commitment to public safety and social justice, but the tightrope she had to walk between appealing to progressives and moderates left some voters unconvinced.

The electoral map in 2024 ultimately reflected these demographic shifts. States like Arizona and Georgia, which had flipped blue in 2020, reverted to Trump in 2024, as he made gains with Latino and rural voters. Meanwhile, Harris struggled to maintain the Democratic coalition that had propelled Biden to victory. States like Pennsylvania and Wisconsin remained fiercely contested, with Trump eking out narrow victories thanks to his strong support in rural areas and among white, working-class voters.

As the polls closed on November 5, 2024, the country braced itself for what many expected to be another drawn-out and contentious vote count. The stakes were incredibly high, and both campaigns had prepared for the possibility of legal battles and recounts in key states. Early returns showed a close race, with Trump performing well in the Midwest and Harris holding her own in key battlegrounds like Georgia and Arizona.

However, as the night wore on, it became clear that Trump was outperforming expectations in several key states. Florida was called for Trump relatively early, with his strong showing among Latino voters in Miami-Dade County and along the Gulf Coast propelling him to victory. Texas also went to Trump, as his dominance in rural areas and the Rio Grande Valley more than offset Harris's gains elsewhere.

The Midwest, once again, became the key to the election. Trump's performance in Michigan, Wisconsin, and Pennsylvania was critical to his path to victory. In these states, Trump's message on the economy, crime, and immigration resonated with working-class voters, many of whom felt that the Democratic Party no longer represented their

interests. Harris won large margins in urban areas like Philadelphia and Detroit, but Trump's dominance in rural regions kept him competitive.

By the early hours of the morning, several networks had projected that Trump would win Wisconsin and Pennsylvania, giving him the necessary electoral votes to secure the presidency. Despite ongoing vote counting in a few states, the momentum was clearly in Trump's favor. The Harris campaign, refusing to concede immediately, called for all votes to be counted, echoing concerns from 2020 about ensuring the integrity of the election. However, Trump declared victory in a speech at his Florida estate, once again asserting that he had saved America from "socialism and chaos."

Donald Trump's victory in 2024 sent shockwaves through the political landscape. His return to the White House marked a dramatic shift in American politics, solidifying the power of the populist right and raising serious questions about the future of the Democratic Party. For Trump's supporters, his win was a vindication of his America First agenda and a rejection of the progressive policies they believed were eroding traditional American values.

However, Trump's victory was met with widespread protests across the country. Many Democratic voters, particularly younger and more progressive activists, saw Trump's second term as a threat to democracy, civil rights, and the environment. In cities like New York, Los Angeles, and Washington,

D.C., similar to 2016 large-scale demonstrations erupted, calling for electoral reforms and condemning Trump's rhetoric.

The Democratic Party, meanwhile, faced a period of soul-searching. Harris's loss, while not a landslide, exposed deep divisions within the party between its progressive and moderate wings. Progressives blamed the loss on the party's failure to energize young and diverse voters, while moderates argued that the common-sense reforms to policing, such as increased accountability, improved training, and the establishment of national standards for use of force. At the same time, Harris emphasized her support for law enforcement and rejected calls from some progressives to defund the police, recognizing the importance of public safety, especially in communities of color that were often disproportionately affected by crime.

The law and order debate was a highly polarizing issue. Trump's base, especially in rural and suburban areas, resonated with his message of restoring order, feeling that their communities were under siege by urban unrest. Trump painted Harris as weak on crime and aligned her with the most radical elements of the Democratic Party, accusing her of supporting the "soft-on-crime" policies of cities like New York, Portland, and Chicago. His campaign successfully linked rising crime rates with what they described as Democratic governance failures, tapping into the fears of voters concerned about safety.

On the other hand, Harris tried to walk a fine line, acknowledging the legitimate concerns of both protestors and law enforcement. She advocated for policies aimed at reducing police violence while also ensuring that public safety remained a priority. However, her nuanced stance often struggled to break through in an election dominated by more extreme rhetoric from both sides. As violence in certain cities continued to make headlines, Trump's message of swift and decisive action seemed to gain more traction with undecided and swing voters.

In states like Wisconsin, Minnesota, and Pennsylvania—where both urban and suburban voters had a direct stake in the law and order debate—the issue became a significant factor in the final stretch of the campaign. Trump's calls for a return to "law and order" were seen as an answer to the perceived chaos, while Harris's message of reform and justice, though popular among younger and more diverse voters, had a harder time convincing older and more conservative-leaning voters.

The media landscape in 2024 was more fragmented and polarized than ever before. Traditional media outlets like CNN, MSNBC, and The New York Times continued to cover the election with a focus on fact-based reporting, but their reach had diminished among large swaths of the population, particularly Trump's supporters. Right-wing media outlets, such as Fox News, One America News Network (OANN), and Newsmax, played a pivotal role in shaping the narrative for Trump's base. These

outlets provided a platform for Trump's message, often amplifying his claims of election fraud, his economic policies, and his attacks on Harris.

Social media, too, was a battleground for narratives, disinformation, and conspiracy theories. Trump's ability to dominate platforms like Facebook, X (formerly Twitter), and Truth Social, his own social media platform, allowed him to bypass traditional media filters and speak directly to his supporters. Despite his ban from certain mainstream platforms following the 2020 election, Trump remained highly visible on the internet, and alternative platforms that catered to conservative voices flourished during the campaign.

One of the most damaging aspects of the 2024 election was the continued spread of misinformation and disinformation, much of it centered around false claims of voter fraud. Trump had never fully conceded the results of the 2020 election, and his 2024 campaign was built, in part, on the promise to "fix" the electoral system. His rallies were filled with claims that the election system was rigged, particularly in Democratic-run cities and states, despite no substantial evidence supporting these claims. Right-wing media and social media networks perpetuated these narratives, making them a central theme of Trump's campaign.

Harris's campaign struggled to combat the spread of false information. While her team worked to correct disinformation and emphasize the importance of trusting the electoral process, the speed and scale at which conspiracy theories spread online made it difficult to keep up. Fact-checking organizations and mainstream news outlets frequently debunked Trump's claims, but for many of Trump's supporters, the media itself was seen as part of the problem, a sentiment Trump had spent years cultivating.

Harris did receive favorable coverage from liberal-leaning outlets like MSNBC and progressive online platforms, but these media ecosystems largely spoke to audiences who were already aligned with her politically. The polarization of media consumption meant that both candidates were, in many ways, preaching to their own choirs, making it difficult for either side to break through to undecided voters.

Voter turnout in 2024 was expected to be high, much like the record-breaking turnout of 2020, but there were important demographic shifts that shaped the outcome of the election. Trump's path to victory relied on maintaining his dominance among white, working-class voters in the Midwest and expanding his support among Latino voters, particularly in states like Florida, Arizona, and Texas. Meanwhile, Harris sought to build a coalition that mirrored Biden's 2020 victory, with strong support from African Americans, young voters, suburban women, and college-educated whites.

However, some key dynamics had shifted since 2020. Trump had made surprising inroads with Latino voters in 2020, particularly in Florida and Texas, and he sought to expand this support in 2024. His message of economic opportunity, combined with his opposition to socialism and his hardline stance on law and order, resonated with more conservative Latino voters, especially Cuban Americans in Florida and Mexican Americans in the Rio Grande Valley. These voters, many of whom had been turned off by the Democratic Party's progressive wing, saw Trump as a defender of traditional values and economic freedom.

At the same time, Harris's campaign worked to mobilize African American and young voters, but turnout in these key demographics did not reach the historic levels seen in 2020. While Harris remained popular among these groups, her appeal did not generate the same level of enthusiasm that Biden had in 2020, particularly in key battleground states and with men. The Democratic Party's failure to fully address issues like police reform and student debt alienated younger progressive voters, who saw Harris as too closely aligned with the establishment.

Suburban women, a key demographic that had swung toward Biden in 2020, were once again a battleground. While Trump had struggled with this group in his previous campaign due to his divisive rhetoric and handling of the COVID-19 pandemic, his law-and-order message resonated with some suburban voters concerned about crime and safety. Harris's campaign worked to counter this by emphasizing her own commitment to public safety and social justice, but the tightrope she had to walk between appealing to progressives and moderates left some voters unconvinced.

The electoral map in 2024 ultimately reflected these demographic shifts. States like Arizona and Georgia, which had flipped blue in 2020, reverted to Trump in 2024, as he made gains with Latino and rural voters. Meanwhile, Harris struggled to maintain the Democratic coalition that had propelled Biden to victory. States like Pennsylvania and Wisconsin remained fiercely contested, with Trump eking out

narrow victories thanks to his strong support in rural areas and among white, working-class voters.

As the polls closed on November 5, 2024, the country braced itself for what many expected to be another drawn-out and contentious vote count. The stakes were incredibly high, and both campaigns had prepared for the possibility of legal battles and recounts in key states. Early returns showed a close race, with Trump performing well in the Midwest and Harris holding her own in key battlegrounds like Georgia and Arizona.

However, as the night wore on, it became clear that Trump was outperforming expectations in several key states. Florida was called for Trump relatively early, with his strong showing among Latino voters in Miami-Dade County and along the Gulf Coast propelling him to victory. Texas also went to Trump, as his dominance in rural areas more than offset Harris's gains in the state's urban centers.

The Midwest, once again, became the key to the election. Trump's performance in Michigan, Wisconsin, and Pennsylvania was critical to his path to victory. In these states, Trump's message on the economy, crime, and immigration resonated with working-class voters, many of whom felt that the Democratic Party no longer represented their interests. Harris won large margins in urban areas like Philadelphia and Detroit, but Trump's dominance in rural and exurban regions kept him competitive. Harris did not connect as Biden had.

By the early hours of the morning, several networks had projected that Trump would win Wisconsin and Pennsylvania, giving him the necessary electoral votes to secure the presidency. Despite ongoing vote counting in a few states, the momentum was clearly in Trump's favor. The Harris campaign, refusing to concede immediately, called for all votes to be counted, echoing concerns from 2020 about ensuring the integrity of the election. However, Trump declared victory in a speech at his Florida estate, once again asserting that he had saved America from "socialism and chaos."

Donald Trump's victory in 2024 sent shockwaves through the political landscape. His return to the White House marked a dramatic shift in American politics, solidifying the power of the populist right and raising serious questions about the future of the

Democratic Party. For Trump's supporters, his win was a vindication of his America First agenda and a rejection of the progressive policies they believed were eroding traditional American values.

However, Trump's victory was met with widespread protests across the country. Many Democratic voters, particularly younger and more progressive activists, saw Trump's second term as a threat to democracy, civil rights, and the environment. In cities like New York, LA, and D.C., large-scale demonstrations erupted, calling for electoral reforms and condemning Trump's rhetoric.

The Democratic Party, meanwhile, faced a period of soul-searching. Harris's loss, while not a landslide, exposed deep divisions within the party between its progressive and moderate wings. Progressives blamed the loss on the party's failure to energize young and diverse voters, while moderates argued that the Democratic Party had drifted too far left, alienating key swing voters in suburban and rural areas. These internal tensions set the stage for a contentious battle over the party's future direction. Many within the party began calling for new leadership, arguing that the establishment figures like Joe Biden, Kamala Harris, and Nancy Pelosi no longer represented the diverse and rapidly changing base of the Democratic electorate.

Donald Trump's return to the White House in January 2025 was marked by a triumphant inaugural address that reflected his populist platform and combative style. He portrayed his victory as a "second chance" to finish the work he started in his first term. With Republicans maintaining control of the House and a slim majority in the Senate, Trump entered office with a stronger mandate to push through his legislative agenda than he had during his first term. His priorities include further deregulation, tax cuts, and a new focus on border security.

However, Trump's second term was not without challenges. The country was more divided than ever, and Trump's rhetoric, which had alienated many voters during his first term, had only intensified. His administration faced resistance not only from Democratic lawmakers but also from within federal agencies and state governments, particularly in blue states. Many cities continued to resist Trump's immigration policies, with mayors of sanctuary cities vowing to defy any federal efforts to round up and deport undocumented immigrants.

On the international stage, Trump's return to power is being met with apprehension by U.S. allies and adversaries alike. His "America First" foreign policy, which had led to strained relationships with traditional allies during his first term, returned in full force. Trump immediately withdrew the U.S. from several international agreements that the Biden administration had re-entered, including the Paris Climate Accord, signaling a sharp pivot away from multilateral diplomacy. In contrast, Trump sought to build on the economic and diplomatic relationships he had forged with authoritarian leaders like

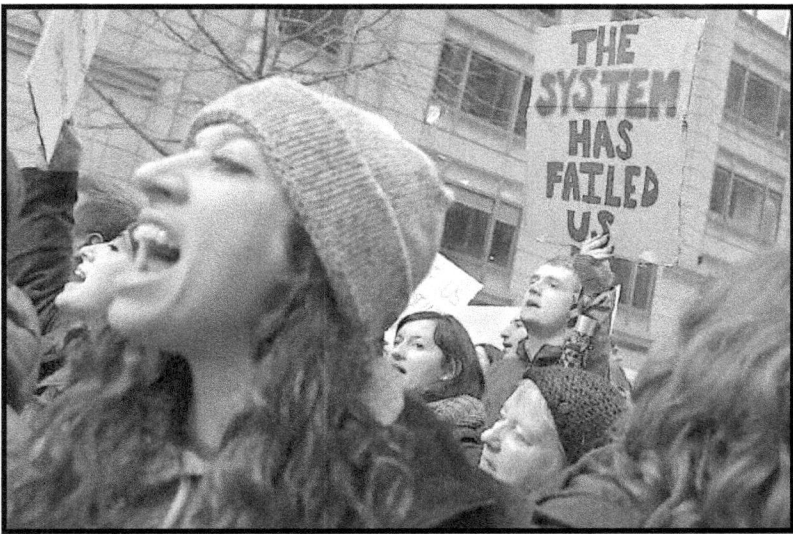

Russia's Vladimir Putin and North Korea's Kim Jong-un.

On domestic issues, Trump moved quickly to roll back key environmental regulations and reintroduce policies that prioritized fossil fuel production. His administration also pushed for more aggressive measures to clamp down on immigration, including the completion of the border wall and stricter rules for asylum seekers. Trump's executive orders on these issues sparked numerous lawsuits, and state governments, especially those led by Democratic governors, mounted legal challenges to many of his policies.

Despite the opposition, Trump remained focused on fulfilling his campaign promises, particularly on the economy. He renewed his commitment to lowering taxes and reducing government regulation, believing that these measures would spur job growth and boost the economy. Although Trump took credit for

111

a booming stock market, the overall economic picture was more complicated. The inflationary pressures that had begun under the Biden administration continued to impact everyday Americans, particularly in the housing and energy markets.

Trump's tax cuts, which benefited corporations and wealthy individuals, were criticized by Democrats as exacerbating income inequality. However, Trump's supporters, particularly in rural and working-class areas, largely viewed his economic policies as beneficial, crediting him with bringing back jobs and protecting American industries.

Trump's victory in 2024 further cemented his dominance over the Republican Party, but it also raised questions about the long-term future of the GOP. While Trump's populist platform energized a significant portion of the electorate, it also alienated more moderate Republicans who were uncomfortable with his divisive rhetoric and focus on culture wars.

In the wake of the election, the Republican Party was increasingly divided between the pro-Trump faction and a smaller, but vocal group of traditional conservatives who were critical of Trump's influence. Figures like Mitt Romney, Liz Cheney, and Adam Kinzinger, who had opposed Trump's leadership, found themselves further marginalized within the party. However, the pro-Trump faction, which included rising stars like Florida Governor

Ron DeSantis and South Dakota Governor Kristi Noem, had fully embraced Trumpism as the future of the party.

As Trump's second term progressed, the question of succession became a topic of intense speculation within Republican circles. While Trump remained the undisputed leader of the GOP, his age and the ongoing legal battles surrounding his previous presidency led many to wonder who would carry the torch once he left office. Figures like DeSantis and Noem, who had skillfully positioned themselves as loyal Trump allies while maintaining their own political profiles, were seen as potential heirs to the Trump legacy.

At the same time, the GOP faced a demographic challenge. Trump's base was overwhelmingly white, older, and rural—demographics that were shrinking as the country became more diverse and urbanized. While Trump had made gains with Latino voters and expanded the Republican coalition in some areas, particularly in Texas and Florida, these gains were not enough to offset the party's long-term challenges. As suburban areas and younger voters continued to trend toward the Democrats, the GOP faced a identity crisis.

For the Democratic Party, the 2024 election loss prompted a period of deep introspection and re-evaluation. The party's internal divisions, which had been papered over during the Biden-Harris administration, came to the forefront in the wake of Trump's victory. Progressives blamed the party's loss on its failure to embrace bold policies, while moderates argued that the party had moved too far to the left, alienating key swing voters in the process.

This internal conflict set the stage for a fierce battle for control of the Democratic Party. On one side, figures like Alexandria Ocasio-Cortez and Bernie Sanders called for the party to embrace a more progressive agenda, focusing on issues like Medicare for All, climate change, and income inequality. On the other side, moderates like Amy Klobuchar and Pete Buttigieg argued for a more centrist approach that could appeal to a broader coalition of voters, particularly in swing states.

The leadership of the Democratic Party was also in question. With Joe Biden retired and Kamala Harris

having lost the election, there was no clear heir apparent. Younger, progressive leaders like Ocasio-Cortez had a strong following among the party's base but were seen as too radical by many moderates. Meanwhile, more centrist figures like Buttigieg and Michigan Governor Gretchen Whitmer positioned themselves as the future of the party, arguing that Democrats needed to find a way to win back working-class voters... mostly in the Midwest and South.

The 2026 midterm elections would prove to be a crucial test for the Democratic Party. With Republicans in control of the presidency and Congress, Democrats would need to unify and develop a coherent message if they hoped to make gains in the House and Senate. The party's ability to balance its progressive and moderate wings would be critical to its success in the coming years.

As Trump's second term unfolded, it became clear that his legacy would be one of profound division. His victory in 2024 had further polarized an already divided nation, with the gap between red and blue states growing ever wider. While Trump's supporters saw him as a champion of American values and a defender of the country's sovereignty, his opponents viewed him as a dangerous demagogue who threatened the very foundations of democracy.

Throughout his second term, Trump faced continued opposition from Democratic lawmakers, the media, and civil society groups. Protests against his policies, particularly on immigration, healthcare, and climate change, continued to flare up across the country. His administration's rollback of environmental regulations and its efforts to repeal key parts of the Affordable Care Act were met with fierce resistance from Democrats.

Trump's relationship with the judiciary also became a focal point of his second term. His administration sought to appoint conservative judges at every level of the federal judiciary, reshaping the courts for decades to come. Trump's ability to appoint multiple Supreme Court justices during his first term had already shifted the balance of the nation's highest court to the right, and his continued appointments solidified conservative control over the judiciary.

Yet, despite the opposition, Trump remained popular with his base. His rallies, which had become a hallmark of his political career, continued to draw tens of thousands of supporters, many of whom saw Trump as a political outsider who was fighting for the "forgotten men and women" of America. His ability to connect with working-class voters and his unfiltered approach to politics ensured that he remained a dominant force within the GOP and American politics more broadly.

As Trump's second term neared its end, the question of his legacy loomed large. Would he be remembered as a transformative figure who reshaped American politics and challenged the establishment? Or would his presidency be seen as a period of intense division and polarization that weakened the country's democratic institutions? The answer would depend largely on the direction the country took after Trump left office.

The 2024 election and Trump's second term underscored the deep divisions within American society. The fault lines that had emerged during his

first presidency—between urban and rural, educated and non-educated, wealthy and working-class—had only deepened. These divisions were not merely political but cultural and ideological, with different segments of the population increasingly living in separate realities, shaped by their media consumption, geography, and social networks.

Trump's presidency represented both a symptom and a cause of this division. His populist message had tapped into the grievances of a large portion of the electorate, particularly those who felt left behind by globalization and cultural change. At the same time, his rhetoric and policies exacerbated the polarization, leading to a political environment in which compromise and consensus seemed increasingly out of reach.

As the country looked toward the future, the challenge for both political parties—and for the nation as a whole—was how to heal these divisions and restore a sense of common purpose. Whether the U.S. would be able to bridge its ideological and cultural divides or whether the country would continue down a path of increasing polarization remained one of the most pressing.

CHAPTER 7

The Spy Glass
The Evolving Media

The role of media in the 2024 presidential election was not only significant but also emblematic of a broader shift in how political discourse is shaped and consumed in the digital age. As with the 2016 and 2020 elections, the media landscape was a battleground where narratives were contested, amplified, and distorted, often in real-time. Traditional news outlets—both broadcast and print —still played a vital role, but their influence had been significantly diluted by the rise of digital platforms, particularly social media, which allowed for more direct and immediate engagement with voters and 'citizen journalists'.

The 2024 election cycle marked a tipping point for the integration of emerging technologies like artificial intelligence (AI) in media, influencing both content creation and distribution. Politicians, media organizations, and voters themselves increasingly relied on algorithms, automated content, and even AI-generated digital news to shape public perceptions. Moreover, the breakdown of the so-called "media gatekeeper" model, where major networks and newspapers dominate the narrative is over.

For both VP Kamala Harris, the Democratic candidate, and Donald Trump, the Republican candidate and former president, the media serve as both a tool for amplification and a minefield of disinformation. Each candidate had a complicated relationship with the media, understanding its power to sway public opinion but also wary of how narratives beyond their control could spiral. The election, therefore, wasn't just a contest of political platforms but also a struggle to dominate media channels and the public discourse they shaped.

In the decades leading up to 2024, the influence of legacy media—traditional outlets like major television networks, print newspapers, and radio—had steadily eroded, but they remained powerful players in shaping the narrative of the election. The dominance of network giants such as CNN, Fox News, and MSNBC continued, though they found themselves competing with newer, digital-first outlets that catered to niche audiences or political extremes. Billions of Ad dollars is on the line.

Fox News, long a stalwart of conservative media, played a pivotal role in galvanizing Donald Trump's base. The network's coverage of Trump was often favorable, framing him as a candidate fighting against political elites, deep state conspiracies, and a liberal media establishment. Fox commentators, like Sean Hannity and Tucker Carlson, who wielded immense influence, are key to perpetuating narratives that support Trump's claims about election integrity, voter fraud, and other hot-button issues. Most of which have been proven false.

Meanwhile, left-leaning outlets like MSNBC and CNN provide counter-programming to Trump's messaging, often framing him as a 'threat to democracy' and amplifying stories that painted the Republican Party as out of touch with mainstream America. These outlets were more favorable to Harris, emphasizing her policy positions on climate change, healthcare, and social justice. Yet, even in their coverage, the tension between progressive and moderate elements within the Democratic Party became a focal point, reflecting the divisions that Harris will need to navigate within her own party.

Print media, led by papers like The New York Times and The Washington Post, still serve as agenda

setters in elections. Investigative reporting from these outlets often broke major stories that shaped public perceptions of both candidates. For instance, in-depth reports on Trump's financial dealings and legal troubles were extensively covered, offering a counter-narrative to his campaign's emphasis on economic growth and populism. On the other side, Harris's record as VP was scrutinized, particularly her handling of immigration and foreign policy.

Despite their reach, legacy media outlets found themselves increasingly sidelined by the explosion of digital platforms that cater to more specific, ideologically homogenous audience. Their once monolithic influence is shattered by the fragmentation of the media ecosystem, where voters can seek out news that reinforces their pre-existing beliefs, creating media silos that further contribute to the polarization of the electorate.

Social media platforms—primarily Facebook, Twitter (now rebranded as X), TikTok, and Instagram—were central to the 2024 election. These platforms not only shaped how voters consumed information in 2024 but also how political campaigns engaged with the electorate. The traditional methods of campaigning—television ads, door-to-door canvassing, and rallies—were still in play, but they were increasingly supplemented by the digital strategies that had become the hallmark of modern political communication.

Donald Trump, who had famously harnessed the power of Twitter in 2016, returned to social media as a primary vehicle for his messaging in 2024, albeit with a different approach after being banned from major platforms in the aftermath of the January 6 Capitol insurrection. His team capitalized on right-wing platforms such as Truth Social, where Trump could speak directly to his supporters without the filters imposed by mainstream outlets. Even with these restrictions, Trump's presence on social media was omnipresent, with his statements and rally clips being widely circulated on platforms like Facebook and X by his supporters and media outlets.

Harris's campaign took a more measured approach to social media, focusing on professional content creation and targeted digital ads. Her team prioritized engagement with younger voters on platforms like TikTok and Instagram, where issues such as climate change, student debt, and reproductive rights dominated the conversation. The

Harris campaign also used data analytics and targeted advertising to reach undecided voters in key battleground states, particularly those who were less likely to consume traditional media.

The rise of TikTok as a political tool was one of the defining features of the 2024 election. Younger voters, many of whom had been politically mobilized by movements such as Black Lives Matter and climate activism, used the platform to create viral content that promoted voter registration, called out disinformation, and highlighted the stark differences between the two candidates. Both campaigns recognized the platform's potential, but Harris had the upper hand, particularly in reaching the under-30 demographic.

However, social media was also a breeding ground for disinformation. In 2024, fake news, conspiracy theories, and deepfakes proliferated, often with devastating consequences. Both foreign and domestic actors leveraged these platforms to spread misleading information, often targeting specific voter groups to suppress turnout or create confusion about voting procedures. Despite efforts by companies like Facebook and X to combat disinformation, their algorithms often prioritized sensational or divisive content, which contributed to the spread of false narratives. The Harris campaign, in particular, had to contend with a barrage of false stories about her record, her background, and even her citizenship, echoing the "birther" conspiracy

theories that had plagued Barack Obama's presidency.

In response to the disinformation crisis, both campaigns engaged in rapid-response efforts to counter false claims. Fact-checking organizations worked in overdrive, but their efforts were often drowned out by the sheer volume of disinformation circulating online. The Harris campaign leaned on these fact-checkers to bolster their credibility, while Trump's supporters frequently dismissed them as biased or part of the "fake news" establishment.

Podcasts, YouTube channels, and alternative news outlets became increasingly influential in 2024, offering long-form content and in-depth discussions that were often absent from the quick-hit nature of social media. These platforms gave rise to independent political commentators, many of whom wield significant influence over their audiences swinging public opinion in ways that traditional media can't.

On the right, figures like Ben Shapiro, Joe Rogan, and Steven Crowder use their platforms to champion Trump's candidacy, often framing him as an outsider fighting against a corrupt political system. Rogan, in particular, has a diverse and influential audience, and his interviews with political figures and commentators are a key venue for discussing issues such as free speech, cancel culture, and the role of government. These long-form discussions allowed for more nuanced takes on Trump's candidacy than what was typically found in mainstream media, contributing to his appeal among libertarian-leaning voters and younger men disillusioned with traditional politics.

On the left, progressive voices such as The Young Turks, Pod Save America, and various independent YouTubers promoted Kamala Harris's candidacy, although not without some reservations. The progressive media ecosystem was less unified than its conservative counterpart, with many commentators critical of Harris for not being progressive enough on issues like healthcare and foreign policy. However, these platforms still served as vital tools for reaching disaffected voters who were concerned with issues like climate change, racial justice, and corporate influence in politics.

The rise of alternative media also contributed to the polarization of the electorate. Voters, increasingly turning to niche outlets that aligned with their ideological views. The 2024 election as a referendum on the role of the media itself. Trust in mainstream media has eroded significantly, with many Americans turning to podcasts and YouTube channels for their news and commentary, further fragmenting the national conversation.

Media bias was a central theme of the 2024 presidential election, with both campaigns accusing the other side of manipulating the media to their advantage. The question of whether mainstream outlets were biased—either toward Harris or Trump—became a defining issue in the campaign.

For Trump's supporters, media bias was a key component of the narrative that the "establishment" was against him. Fox News, despite being a conservative network, faced criticism from some of Trump's most ardent supporters for not being loyal enough to the former president. Trump himself frequently railed against the "fake news media," accusing outlets like CNN, ABC and The New York Times of being nothing more than propaganda arms for the Democratic Party. This rhetoric, which had begun during Trump's first presidential run, intensified in 2024, with many voters viewing the media as part of a broader conspiracy to undermine his campaign.

On the Democratic side, Kamala Harris's campaign had its own struggles with media bias. While liberal outlets were generally more favorable to her candidacy, there were still tensions between Harris and certain segments of the media, particularly the progressive press. Outlets like The New York Times and The Washington Post were more supportive of Harris's candidacy, but progressive platforms such as The Intercept and Jacobin critiqued her for not being bold enough on issues like Medicare for All, police reform, and corporate regulation. This tension reflected the broader ideological divide within the Democratic Party, where Harris was seen by some as too moderate to represent the future of the party.

Despite the overall tilt toward Harris in much of the mainstream media, the question of media bias remained a constant undercurrent throughout the campaign. Both candidates used this perception of bias to rally their respective bases—Trump positioned himself as the perpetual underdog fighting against a corrupt media establishment, while Harris emphasized her ability to govern in the face of relentless scrutiny. This dynamic played out on both traditional and social media platforms, where debates over the legitimacy of news sources often overshadowed substantive policy discussions.

The fragmentation of media outlets only served to reinforce this perception of bias. As news consumers increasingly sought information from sources that aligned with their own ideological viewpoints, the notion of an unbiased media became less relevant to many voters. Instead, voters gravitated toward outlets that confirmed their preexisting beliefs, reinforcing political polarization and making it harder for the candidates to reach undecided voters through traditional channels.

Disinformation and the spread of conspiracy theories were among the most troubling features of the 2024 election. With the rise of social media and alternative media outlets, it became easier than ever for false information to circulate widely and rapidly. Both foreign and domestic actors took advantage of this to sow confusion, division, and mistrust.

One of the most pervasive conspiracy theories during the 2024 election was the continuation of the false claims of widespread voter fraud that Trump had advanced in 2020. Despite multiple investigations and court rulings that found no evidence of significant fraud in the previous election, Trump and his supporters continued to promote these claims, amplified by social media networks and right-wing media outlets. This contributed to a persistent distrust in the electoral process among a sizable portion of the electorate.

On the Democratic side, Harris's campaign faced its own share of disinformation. As the first woman of color to be a major party's presidential nominee, she was the target of numerous false and racist claims, many of which spread rapidly on social media platforms. False stories about her record as a prosecutor, her personal background, and even her eligibility to run for president were circulated widely. While Harris's campaign was proactive in countering these falsehoods, the sheer volume of disinformation made it difficult.

Social media platforms like Facebook, X, and TikTok took steps to mitigate the spread of disinformation, but their efforts were often inconsistent and criticized as insufficient. Fact-checking organizations worked around the clock to debunk false claims, but the speed at which disinformation could spread, combined with the deep distrust many voters had in the mainstream media, meant that these efforts were often too little, too late. Foreign interference was also a concern in the 2024 election, though it did not reach the levels seen in 2016. Nevertheless, intelligence agencies warned of foreign actors using disinformation to influence the election, particularly through social media platforms. These efforts were often aimed at exacerbating divisions within the electorate, with the goal of undermining trust in democratic institutions.

The consequences of disinformation in the 2024 election were profound. Many voters, particularly Trump supporters, remained convinced that the electoral process was rigged, regardless of evidence to the contrary. This undermined public confidence in the integrity of the election and raised concerns about the long-term health of American democracy. For Harris, disinformation complicated her efforts to appeal to moderate and undecided voters, who were often bombarded with conflicting narratives that made it difficult to discern the truth. These creators were not bound by the traditional norms of journalism, which allowed them to offer more opinionated and sometimes sensationalized content, but it also meant

they were not subject to the same editorial oversight and fact-checkings.

For the Harris campaign, independent creators provided both opportunities and challenges. On the one hand, many progressive content creators supported her candidacy, using their platforms to mobilize younger voters and promote issues like climate change, reproductive rights, and healthcare reform. On the other hand, the lack of control over messaging meant that Harris's campaign often had to contend with a variety of voices that didn't always align with their official platform.

Trump, meanwhile, continued to thrive in the world of independent media, particularly through right-wing content creators who were sympathetic to his populist message. Many of these creators framed Trump as the champion of free speech and a bulwark against the so-called "cancel culture" of the left. Trump's relationship with independent content creators was symbiotic—while they amplified his message, he provided them with the kind of controversial content that their audiences craved.

Citizen journalism also played a role in covering campaign events and rallies. With smartphones and social media, ordinary people could live-stream or report on events in real-time, bypassing traditional media outlets. This allowed both campaigns to engage more directly with voters but also increased the potential for misinformation.

The rise of independent content creators and citizen journalists signaled a broader shift in the media landscape, where traditional gatekeepers no longer held a monopoly on political information. While this democratization of media allowed for a more diverse range of voices, it also contributed to the fragmentation of the electorate, as voters increasingly turned to sources that reinforced their own beliefs. A self imposed echo chamber.

One of the biggest challenges in the 2024 election was the question of how to regulate media, particularly in the digital space. The rapid growth of social media platforms, independent content creators, and alternative news outlets had outpaced existing regulatory frameworks, leaving policymakers and regulators struggling to keep up.

Efforts to regulate social media companies in the lead-up to the election focused on issues such as disinformation, hate speech, and foreign interference. Platforms like Facebook and X faced increasing scrutiny from both the public and lawmakers, with some calling for more stringent regulations to prevent the spread of harmful content. However, these efforts are often met with resistance from the platforms themselves, who argued that overly aggressive regulation could stifle free speech and innovation.

The debate over Section 230 of the 2024 Communications Decency Act, which provides legal immunity to social media platforms for content posted by their users, was particularly contentious. Trump and his supporters called for the repeal or reform of Section 230, arguing that it allowed platforms to censor conservative voices. Harris, while also supporting some reforms to Section 230, took a more measured approach, focusing on the need for greater transparency and accountability from tech companies without dismantling the protections that allowed for a free and open internet.

Regulating disinformation proved to be even more challenging. While platforms implemented policies to flag or remove false content, these efforts were often uneven and difficult to enforce. The decentralized nature of the internet made it easy for disinformation to spread across multiple platforms, and bad actors could easily evade detection by using encrypted messaging apps or alternative platforms that operated outside the reach of U.S. regulators.

Another challenge was the question of media consolidation. In the years leading up to 2024, major

media companies had consolidated their power through mergers and acquisitions, leading to concerns about the concentration of ownership in the hands of a few large corporations. This raised questions about the diversity of viewpoints in the media and the ability of smaller, independent outlets to compete in a more monopolistic environment.

The Harris campaign, like many Democrats today, supported policies aimed at breaking up media monopolies and promoting greater competition in the marketplace of ideas. However, these efforts were complicated by the fact that many of the most popular alternative media outlets were digital platforms that operated outside the traditional regulatory framework.

The role of government in regulating media in the digital age remained a divisive issue in the 2024 election, with both sides grappling with the tension between promoting free speech and curbing the harmful effects of disinformation. As the media landscape continued to evolve, it was clear that new regulatory approaches would be needed to address the unique challenges of the 21st-century information ecosystem.

The 2024 presidential election underscored the complex and evolving relationship between the media and American politics. As traditional media continued to lose influence to digital platforms, social media, and independent creators, the way in which voters consumed information—and the way campaigns communicated with the electorate— fundamentally changed.

Looking ahead, the role of media in American politics will likely continue to grow more fragmented and polarized. The rise of alternative media outlets, the proliferation of disinformation, and the increasing dominance of social media platforms will present both opportunities and challenges for future candidates. While digital platforms offer a more direct way to reach voters, they also contribute to the echo chambers that have deepened political divisions in the country.

For the American electorate, the 2024 election raised important questions about the future of democracy in the digital age. As voters become increasingly skeptical of mainstream media, and as disinformation becomes more pervasive, the challenge will be how to ensure that citizens have access to accurate and reliable information

<u>Epilogue</u>

The 2024 Presidential Election was one for the history books! As I write this at 11pm on election night approximately 165 million of the 244 million eligible citizens voted. Early voting began in Oct. and in 4 states even began in September. A growing number, 31% of voters polled say they prefer to vote via mail in absentee ballot. More than 88Million voters voted early either in person or by mail.

Both campaigns spent the last few hours out in the streets trying to reach the 270 electoral votes to win. According to the US Election Assistance Commission approximately 100,000 few polling places were available during the 2024 election cycle. And outside political ad spending surpassed more than $3 billion the most in history.

ELECTION NIGHT Nov. 5, 2024
Timeline

We go into election day with Harris and Trump in a statistical dead heat! By all accounts it looks to be the closest race in American History More than 78 million Americans voted early either in person or by mail. Last night Trump ended his campaign in NC while Harris continues to campaign. The seven battle starts that will deicide the election are: MI, PA, NC, WIS, GA, AZ, NV Most are projecting that it's either PA or MI that will help a candidate reach 270 electoral votes and the White House. For media coverage we are monitoring; CNN, Fox, ABC and other media outlets.

6am: Media Electoral Prediction =
        HARRIS= 319
        TRUMP = 219

Midnight: The first vote is cast in Dixville Notch, New Hampshire

7am est: - Polls Open!

9am: Turn out appears to be high. America holds its breath.

Noon: In line for almost 90 minutes and lines at most polling stations. It appears to be a heavy voting turn out.

3pm: Early indicators show Trump making early inroads in all counts. Forecasts say it is the closest race in American history.

6pm: Four of the seven battle ground states show Trump ahead. GOP takes the US Senate.

9pm: Polls start to close with first results coming in. GOP surging ahead.

10pm: Trump takes all of the 'Blue Wall' states; Wis., Mich. and PA.

11pm: The House of Representatives is still too close to call.

Midnight:
Media reports Semi-Final Electoral College =
Trump - 292
Harris - 224

2am 11/6: Former President Trump declares victory in a speech from West Palm Beach, FL

Nov. 6, 2pm; Vice President Harris concedes in a speech at her college alma mater Howard University. She calls for unity and working together to find common ground. The Democratic Party immediately goes into the blame game.

As Election Day 2024 is written into the history books there was no civil unrest and things went smoothly. One thing is certain… America has taken a definite turn towards the right. But all was and is quite in the USA! The election will certified by the electoral college and then of course there is the presidential inaugural on the mall… all of which is ripe for civil unrest justified or not. It is only hoped that cooler heads and patriotism will prevail.

We wish President-Elect Trump our congratulations and our best hopes and prayers for a successful administration.

So who won? Ultimately it was the American people. Millions of American's voted in the 2024 election the real testament to our nation's perseverance. One of the highest levels of voter participation in history. Despite the doom and gloom and predictions of Civil War and fighting in the streets the union still stands and the Stars and Stripes still flies above… long may it wave!

VOTE

<u>Acknowledgments</u>

The Democratic Party

The Republican Party

League of Women Voters

PollWatch USA

U.S. Election Assistance Commission

National Association of Nonpartisan Reformers
https://nonpartisanreformers.org

Nonprofit Vote
https://www.nonprofitvote.org

Ballotpedia
https://ballotpedia.org

Brennan Center for Justice
https://www.brennancenter.org

Vote Smart
https://justfacts.votesmart.org

https://www.ncsl.org/elections-and-campaigns/poll-watchers-and-challengers

<u>Please Leave a Review!</u>

A Small Ask...

Now that you've finished reading this book, what do you think of what you read? Are there any tips or information you found insightful? What do you think is missing from this book? While you're thinking back on what you read, it'd mean the world to me if you left an honest review on Amazon.

As you probably know, reviews play a part in building relevancy for all products on Amazon. Whether you found the information helpful or worthless, your candid review helps other customers make an informed purchase.
Also, based on your review, I'll adjust this publication and future editions.

I appreciate your support!

Goodreads Author

Now Available

•Book

•eBook

Coming Soon!
•Audiobook
On Audible

www.authortommcauliffe.com

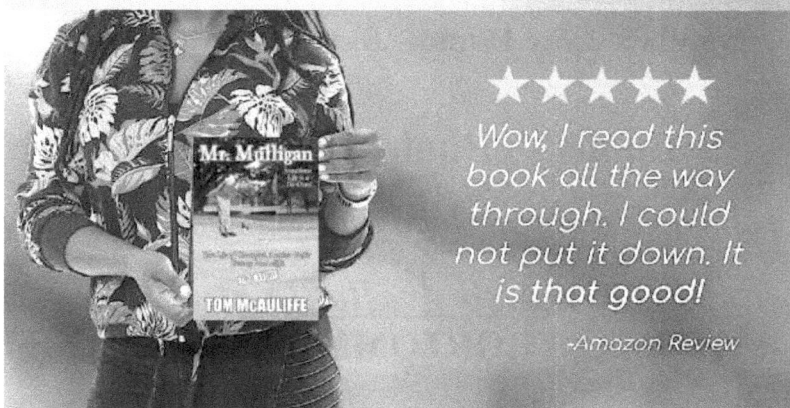

OFF THE ROCK
Escaping Alcatraz

Tom McAuliffe

•Kindle

•Apple

•BaM

•Barns & Noble

•Amazon

•Smash words

Books by Author Tom McAuliffe

- **Mr. Mulligan** - *The Life of Champion Armless Golfer Tommy McAuliffe*

- **Nuts!** - *The Life & Times of Gen. Tony McAuliffe*

- **Throttle Up** - *Astronaut Teacher Christa McAuliffe*

- **Mad Dog!** - *Detroit Tiger Dick McAuliffe*

- **Charmed** - *From Motown to Combat & Back*

- **Almost** - *The Road to the Grande*

- **Thunder Road** - *Goodyear, God & Gatorade*

- **Buddy, Brian and Me** - *A Spooky Rock Story*

- **Frozen** - *A WWII and Mind over Matter Tale*

- **Soft Shell** - *Teddy the Talking Turtle*

- **Max and Me** - *Paws Across The Water*

- **Off the Rock** - *Escaping Alcatraz*

- **Deepwater Oil** - *Drillin on the Moon*

- **No Place Like Home** - *The No BS Real Estate Guide*

Books - eBooks - Audio Books
On sale at Amazon, Kindle, Apple Books, Barnes & Noble and your local independent book store!

Also Available at:
WWW.AUTHORTOMMCAULIFFE.COM

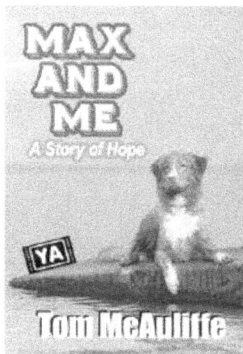

MAX AND ME
A Story of Hope
YA
Tom McAuliffe

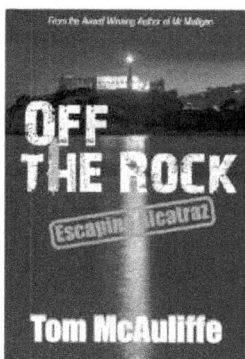

From the Award Winning Author of Mr. Mulligan
OFF THE ROCK
Escaping Alcatraz
Tom McAuliffe

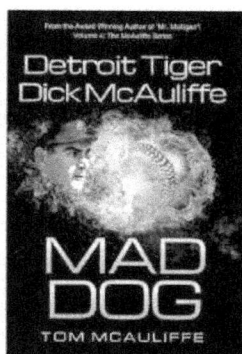

From the Award Winning Author of Mr. Mulligan!
Volume 4: The McAuliffe Series
Detroit Tiger
Dick McAuliffe
MAD DOG
TOM MCAULIFFE

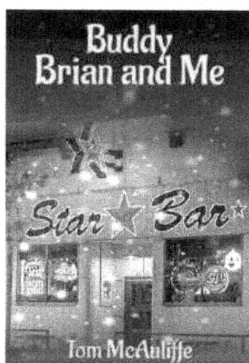

Buddy
Brian and Me
Star Bar
Tom McAuliffe

SOFT SHELL
TEDDY THE TALKING TURTLE
YA
Tom McAuliffe

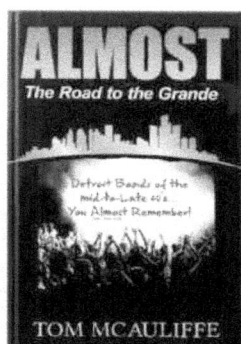

ALMOST
The Road to the Grande
Detroit Bands of the
mid-to-Late 60's
You Almost Remember!
TOM MCAULIFFE

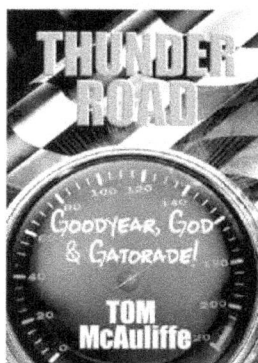

THUNDER ROAD
GOODYEAR, GOD
& GATORADE!
TOM McAuliffe

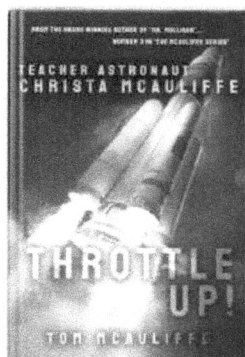

FROM THE AWARD WINNING AUTHOR OF "MR. MULLIGAN"...
BOOK 3 IN "THE McAULIFFE SERIES"
TEACHER ASTRONAUT
CHRISTA MCAULIFFE
THROTTLE UP!
TOM MCAULIFFE

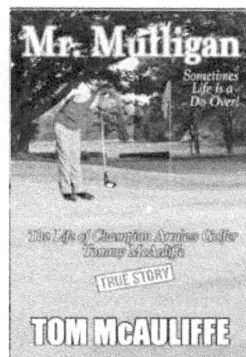

Mr. Mulligan
Sometimes
Life is a
Do Over!
The Life of Champion Amateur Golfer
Tommy McAuliffe
TRUE STORY
TOM MCAULIFFE

FROZEN
A WWII Mind Over Matter Tale
Tom McAuliffe
From the Award Winning Author of "Mr. Mulligan"

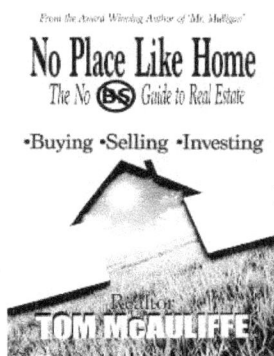

From the Award Winning Author of "Mr. Mulligan"
No Place Like Home
The No BS Guide to Real Estate
•Buying •Selling •Investing
Realtor
TOM MCAULIFFE

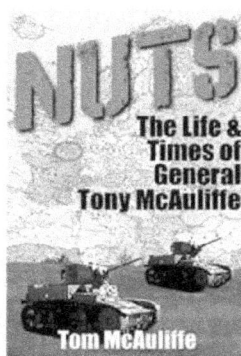

NUTS
The Life &
Times of
General
Tony McAuliffe
Tom McAuliffe

100% HUMAN CREATED CONTENT

COPYRIGHT LAW
FAIR USE
COPYRIGHT LAW

www.ingramcontent.com/pod-product-compliance
Lightning Source LLC
Chambersburg PA
CBHW060937040426
42445CB00011B/898